LANDMARK DECISIONS OF THE UNITED STATES SUPREME COURT IV

MAUREEN HARRISON & STEVE GILBERT
EDITORS

THE LANDMARK DECISIONS SERIES

EXCELLENT BOOKS
SAN DIEGO, CALIFORNIA

EXCELLENT BOOKS
Post Office Box 131322
Carlsbad, CA 92013-1322

"This publication is designed to provide accurate and authoritative information in regard to the subject matter covered. It is sold with the understanding that the publisher is not engaged in rendering legal or other professional service. If legal advice or other expert assistance is required, the services of a competent professional person should be sought." - From a Declaration of Principles jointly adopted by a Committee of the American Bar Association and a Committee of Publishers.

Publisher's Cataloging in Publication Data

Landmark Decisions Of The United States Supreme Court IV/
  Maureen Harrison, Steve Gilbert, editors.
  p. cm. - (Landmark Decisions Series)
Bibliography:p.
Includes Index.

1. United States. Supreme Court.
I. Title. II. Harrison, Maureen. III. Gilbert, Steve.
IV. Series: Landmark Decisions Series.

KF8742.H24 1994   LC 90-84578
347.'73'26-dc20
[347.30726]
ISBN 0-9628014-7-X

INTRODUCTION

When we have examined in detail the organization of the Supreme Court, and the entire prerogatives which it exercises, we shall readily admit that a more imposing judicial power was never constituted by any people.

Alexis de Tocqueville
Democracy In America (1835)

The United States Supreme Court exercises what de Tocqueville termed its "imposing judicial power" to settle all Constitutional controversies. Justice Benjamin Cardozo wrote: "The sordid controversies of litigants are the stuff out of which great and shining truths will ultimately be shaped." The "sordid controversies" of ordinary individuals like Jane Roe, Ernesto Miranda, Linda Brown, and Homer Plessy, and extraordinary individuals like John D. Rockefeller, Richard Nixon, and Muhammad Ali have all, at one time or another, found their way before the United States Supreme Court to become Justice Cardozo's stuff out of which truths are shaped.

These "truths" become legal precedents. Justice Cardozo explained: "It will not do to decide the same question one way between one set of litigants and the opposite way between another." Once a legal precedent is established in a Supreme Court decision, it can stand undisturbed for all time, as has the 1819 *McCulloch* Federal Supremacy decision. It may be overturned by a new Court, as was the 1896 *Plessy* Separate But Equal decision by the 1954 *Brown* School Desegregation decision. Or it may be overturned by the Congress, as was the 1819 *Dagenhart* Child Labor decision by the 1938 Fair Labor Standards Act. Finally, it may be overturned by the States themselves, as was the 1857 *Dred Scott* Slavery decision by the Fourteenth Amendment to the United States Constitution.

Only the Court has the authority to construct and interpret the meaning of the Constitution. Every year over five thousand requests for review of lower court decisions are received by the Court. Requests, called petitions for *certiorari,* come to the Court from the losing side in Federal Appeals or State Supreme Courts. Four of the nine Justices must agree to a review. Only four hundred cases are accepted each year. Once accepted, written arguments, called briefs, pro and con, are submitted to the Court by both the petitioner, the side appealing the lower court decision against them, and the respondent, the side defending the lower court decision in their favor. Interested parties, called *amici curiae* [friends of the Court], may be permitted to file their own briefs in support of either side. After briefs are submitted to and reviewed by the Justices, public oral arguments are heard by the Court. Lawyers for the petitioner and respondent are allowed thirty minutes to make their case before the Justices. The Justices, at their discretion, may interrupt at any time to require further explanations, to pose hypothetical questions, or make observations.

Twice a week, on Wednesday and Friday, the Justices meet alone in conference to discuss each case and to vote on the outcome. They may affirm [uphold] or reverse [change the outcome of], in whole or in part, the decisions of the lower courts from which these appeals have come. One Justice, voting in the majority, will be selected to write the majority opinion. In rare instances the Court will issue its decision *per curiam* [by the Court majority without attribution of authorship]. Justices may join in the majority opinion, write their own concurring opinion, write their own dissenting opinion, or join in another's concurrence or dissent. Drafts of the majority, concurring, and dissenting opinions circulate among the Justices for their comments. Opinions are redrafted and recirculated until a consensus is reached and a carefully worded decision is announced. It is the majority decision that stands as the law of the land.

Judge Learned Hand wrote: "The language of the law must not be foreign to the ears of those who are to obey it." The twelve Landmark Decisions presented in this book are carefully edited versions of the official texts issued by the Supreme Court in *United States Reports*. We, as editors, have made every effort to replace esoteric legalese with plain English without damaging the original decisions. Edited out are long alpha-numeric legal citations and wordy wrangles over points of procedure. Edited in are definitions (*writ of habeas corpus* = an order from a judge to bring a person to court), translations (*certiorari* = the decision of the Court to review a case), identifications (Appellant = Homer Plessy, Appellee = Judge John Ferguson), and explanations (where the case originated, how it got to the court, what the issues were, and who the parties were).

You will find in this book the majority opinion of the Court as expressed by the Justice chosen to speak for the Court. Also included are selected dissenting opinions of Justices opposed to the majority. Preceding each edited decision, we note where the complete decision can be found. The bibliography provides a list of further reading on the cases and the Court. Also included for the reader's reference is a complete copy of the United States Constitution, to which every decision refers.

Justice Oliver Wendell Holmes, Jr. wrote: We are very quiet here, but it is the quiet of a storm center. . . ." *Landmark Decisions of the United States Supreme Court* is edited for all those who want to stand in the center of America's legal storms.

M.H. & S.G.

This book is dedicated to our sister,

Susan

TABLE OF CONTENTS

SEPARATE BUT EQUAL
75

If the civil and political rights of both races be equal, one cannot be inferior to the other civilly or politically. If one race be inferior to the other socially, the Constitution of the United States cannot put them upon the same plane.

Justice Henry Brown
Plessy v. Ferguson (1896)

90

Our Constitution is color-blind, and neither knows nor tolerates classes among its citizens. In respect of civil rights, all citizens are equal before the law.... The law regards a man as a man, and takes no account ... of his color when his civil rights as guaranteed by the supreme law of the land are involved.

Justice John Marshall Harlan
Dissenting in *Plessy*

TRUST BUSTING
105

As substantial power over the crude product was the inevitable result of the absolute control which existed over the refined product, the monopolization of the one carried with it the power to control the other.

Chief Justice Edward Douglas White
Standard Oil v. United States (1911)

CHILD LABOR
115

The control by Congress over interstate commerce cannot authorize the exercise of authority not intrusted to it by the Constitution.

Justice William Rufus Day
Hammer v. Dagenhart (1918)

THE ATOMIC SPIES
125

Our liberty is maintained only so long as justice is secure. To permit our judicial processes to be used to obstruct the course of justice destroys our freedom. . . . Though the penalty is great and our responsibility heavy, our duty is clear.

> Justice Tom Clark
> *The Rosenbergs v. United States (1953)*

130

[W]here two penal statutes apply - one carrying death, the other imprisonment - the court has no choice but to impose the less harsh sentence.

> Justice William O. Douglas
> Dissenting in *The Rosenbergs*

LIBEL
135

'The First Amendment presupposes that right conclusions are more likely to be gathered out of a multitude of tongues, than through any kind of authoritative selection. To many this is, and always will be, folly; but we have staked upon it our all.'

> Justice William Brennan
> *The New York Times v. Sullivan (1964)*

CONSCIENTIOUS OBJECTION
159

In order to qualify for classification as a conscientious objector, a registrant must satisfy three basic tests. He must show he is conscientiously opposed to war in any form. He must show that this opposition is based upon religious training and belief. . . . And he must show that this objection is sincere.

> *Muhammad Ali v. United States (1971)*

HATE CRIMES
167

Let there be no mistake about our belief that burning a cross in someone's front yard is reprehensible. But St. Paul has sufficient means at its disposal to prevent such behavior without adding the First Amendment to the fire.

Justice Antonin Scalia
R.A.V. v. St. Paul (1992)

179

The Wisconsin statute singles out for [penalty] enhancement bias-motivated conduct because this conduct is thought to inflict greater individual and societal harm. . . . [B]ias-motivated crimes are more likely to provoke retaliatory crimes, inflict emotional harms on their victims, and incite community unrest.

Chief Justice William Rehnquist
Wisconsin v. Mitchell (1993)

U.S. CONSTITUTION
187

BIBLIOGRAPHY
217

INDEX
223

FEDERAL SUPREMACY

McCulloch v. Maryland

The Constitution, and the laws of the United States which shall be made in pursuance thereof . . . shall be the supreme law of the land; and the judges in every state shall be bound thereby, anything in the Constitution or laws of any state to the contrary notwithstanding.

The Supremacy Clause of the U.S. Constitution

In 1816 Congress, under authority of the Constitution, created The Second Bank of the United States. The Bank, the Government's fiscal agent and depository, opened twenty-five branches in several states to compete with state banks. These included a branch in Baltimore, Maryland.

The Bank, seen by many to be controlled by Eastern commercial interests, was poorly managed. In August 1818, The Bank caused a financial panic by recalling all its loans and accepting only gold, silver, or its own notes in payment. Many state banks failed in the Panic of 1819 and a nationwide depression followed.

In reaction Maryland, asserting a states rights argument that the Constitution gave Congress no specific powers to create The Bank, enacted a tax to destroy it. The Bank, maintaining the Constitution's Supremacy Clause (Article Six, Clause Two) gave Congress implied powers to create it, refused to pay. Maryland sued The Bank in the person of their Baltimore cashier, James McCulloch. The State prevailed in Baltimore County Court, the Maryland Court of Appeals, and the Maryland Supreme Court. McCulloch appealed to the United States Supreme Court.

Oral arguments commenced on February 22, 1819, with Daniel Webster representing The Bank and Maryland Attorney General Luther Martin representing the State. On March 6, 1819 Chief Justice John Marshall announced the 7-0 decision of the Court. The edited text follows.

THE McCULLOCH COURT

Chief Justice John Marshall
Appointed by President John Adams
Served 1801 - 1835

Associate Justice Bushrod Washington
Appointed by President John Adams
Served 1789 - 1829

Associate Justice William Johnson
Appointed by President Jefferson
Served 1804 - 1834

Associate Justice Thomas Todd
Appointed by President Jefferson
Served 1807 - 1826

Associate Justice Joseph Story
Appointed by President Madison
Served 1811 - 1845

Associate Justice Gabriel Duval
Appointed by President Madison
Served 1811 - 1835

Associate Justice Smith Thompson
Appointed by President Monroe
Served 1823 - 1826

The unedited text of *McCulloch v. Maryland* can be found
on page 316, volume 17 of *United States Reports.*

McCULLOCH v. MARYLAND
MARCH 6, 1819

CHIEF JUSTICE MARSHALL: In the case now to be determined, the defendant [Maryland], a sovereign state, denies the obligation of a law enacted by the legislature of the Union, and the plaintiff [McCulloch], on his part, contests the validity of an act which has been passed by the legislature of that state. The constitution of our country, in its most interesting and vital parts, is to be considered; the conflicting powers of the government of the Union and of its members, as marked in that constitution, are to be discussed; and an opinion given, which may essentially influence the great operations of the government. No tribunal can approach such a question without a deep sense of its importance, and of the awful responsibility involved in its decision. But it must be decided peacefully, or remain a source of hostile legislation, perhaps of hostility of a still more serious nature; and if it is to be so decided, by this tribunal alone can the decision be made. On the Supreme Court of the United States has the constitution of our country devolved this important duty.

The first question . . . is, has Congress power to incorporate a bank?

It has been truly said that this can scarcely be considered as an open question, entirely unprejudiced by the former proceedings of the nation respecting it. The principle now contested was introduced at a very early period of our history, has been recognized by many successive legislatures, and has been acted upon by the judicial department, in cases of peculiar delicacy, as a law of undoubted obligation.

. . . . The power now contested was exercised by the first Congress elected under the present constitution. The bill for incorporating the [First B]ank of the United States did not steal upon an unsuspecting legislature, and pass unobserved. Its principle was completely understood, and was opposed with equal zeal and ability. After being resisted, first in the fair and open field of debate, and afterwards in the executive cabinet, with as much persevering talent as any measure has ever experienced, and being supported by arguments which convinced minds as pure and as intelligent as this country can boast, it became a law. The original act was permitted to expire; but a short experience of the embarrassments to which the refusal to revive it exposed the government, convinced those who were most prejudiced against the measure of its necessity and induced the passage of the present law. It would require no ordinary share of intrepidity to assert that a measure adopted under these circumstances was a bold and plain usurpation, to which the constitution gave no countenance.

. . . . The powers of the general government, it has been said, are delegated by the states, who alone are truly sovereign; and must be exercised in subordination to the states, who alone possess supreme dominion.

It would be difficult to sustain [maintain] this proposition. The convention which framed the constitution was indeed elected by the state legislatures. But the instrument, when it came from their hands, was a mere proposal, without obligation, or pretensions to it. It was reported to the then existing Congress of the United States, with a request that it might "be submitted to a convention of delegates, chosen in each state by the people thereof, under the recommendation of its legislature, for their assent and ratification." This mode of proceeding was adopted; and by the convention, by Congress, and by the state legislatures, the instrument was submitted to the people. They acted upon it in the only manner in which they can act safely, effectively, and wisely, on such a subject, by assembling in convention. It is true, they assembled in their several states - and where else should they have assembled? No political dreamer was ever wild enough to think of breaking down the lines which separate the states, and of compounding the American people into one common mass. Of consequence, when they act, they act in their states. But the measures they adopt do not, on that account, cease to be the measures of the people themselves, or become the measures of the state governments.

From these conventions the constitution derives its whole authority. The government proceeds directly from the people; is "ordained and established" in the name of the people; and is declared to be ordained, "in order to form a more perfect union, establish justice, insure domestic tranquillity, and secure the blessings of liberty to themselves and to their posterity." The assent of the states, in their sovereign capacity, is implied in calling a convention, and thus submitting that instrument to the people. But the people were at perfect liberty to accept or reject it; and their act was final. It required not the affirmance, and could not be negatived, by the state governments. The constitution, when thus adopted, was of complete obligation, and bound the state sovereignties.

It has been said that the people had already surrendered all their powers to the state sovereignties, and had nothing more to give. But, surely, the question whether they may resume and modify the powers granted to government does not remain to be settled in this country. Much more might the legitimacy of the general government be doubted, had it been created by the states. The powers delegated to the state sovereignties were to be exercised by themselves, not by a distinct and independent sovereignty, created by themselves. To the formation of a league, such as was the confederation, the state sovereignties were certainly competent. But when, "in order to form a more perfect union," it was deemed necessary to change this alliance into an effective government, possessing great and sovereign powers, and acting directly on the people, the necessity of referring it to the people, and of deriving its powers directly from them, was felt and acknowledged by all.

The government of the Union, then (whatever may be the influence of this fact on the case), is, emphatically, and truly, a government of the people. In form and in substance it emanates from them. Its powers are granted by them, and are to be exercised directly on them, and for their benefit.

This government is acknowledged by all to be one of enumerated powers. The principle, that it can exercise only the powers granted to it, would seem too apparent to have required to be enforced by all those arguments which its enlightened friends, while it was depending before the people, found it necessary to urge. That principle is now universally admitted. But the question respecting the extent of the powers actually granted, is perpetually arising, and will probably continue to arise, as long as our system shall exist.

In discussing these questions, the conflicting powers of the general and state governments must be brought into view, and the supremacy of their respective laws, when they are in opposition, must be settled.

If any one proposition could command the universal assent of mankind, we might expect it would be this - that the government of the Union, though limited in its powers, is supreme within its sphere of action. This would seem to result necessarily from its nature. It is the government of all; its powers are delegated by all; it represents all, and acts for all. Though any one state may be willing to control its operations, no state is willing to allow others to control them. The nation, on those subjects on which it can act, must necessarily bind its component parts. But this question is not left to mere reason; the people have, in express terms, decided it by saying, "this constitution, and the laws of the United States, which shall be made in pursuance thereof," "shall be the supreme law of the land," and by requiring that the members of the state legislatures, and the officers of the executive and judicial departments of the states shall take the oath of fidelity to it.

The government of the United States, then, though limited in its powers, is supreme; and its laws, when made in pursuance of the constitution, form the supreme law of the land, "anything in the constitution or laws of any state to the contrary notwithstanding."

Among the enumerated powers, we do not find that of establishing a bank or creating a corporation. But there is no phrase in the instrument which, like the articles of confederation, excludes incidental or implied powers; and which requires that everything granted shall be expressly and minutely described. Even the Tenth Amendment, which was framed for the purpose of quieting the exces-

sive jealousies which had been excited, omits the word
"expressly," and declares only that the powers "not delegated to the United States, nor prohibited to the states, are
reserved to the states or to the people;" thus leaving the
question, whether the particular power which may become
the subject of contest has been delegated to the one government, or prohibited to the other, to depend on a fair
construction of the whole instrument. The men who drew
and adopted this amendment had experienced the embarrassments resulting from the insertion of this word in the
articles of confederation, and probably omitted it to avoid
those embarrassments. A constitution, to contain an accurate detail of all the subdivisions of which its great powers will admit, and of all the means by which they may be
carried into execution, would partake of a prolixity of a
legal code, and could scarcely be embraced by the human
mind. It would probably never be understood by the public. Its nature, therefore, requires, that only its great out-
lines should be marked, its important objects designated,
and the minor ingredients which compose those objects be
deduced from the nature of the objects themselves. That
this idea was entertained by the framers of the American
constitution, is not only to be inferred from the nature of
the instrument, but from the language. Why else were
some of the limitations, found in the ninth section of the
first article, introduced? It is also, in some degree, war-
ranted by their having omitted to use any restrictive term
which might prevent its receiving a fair and just interpretation. In considering this question, then, we must never
forget that it is a constitution we are expounding.

. . . . It is, then, the subject of fair inquiry, how far such
means may be employed. It is not denied that the powers
given to the government imply the ordinary means of execution. That, for example of raising revenue, and apply-

ing it to national purposes, is admitted to imply the power of conveying money from place to place, as the exigencies of the nation may require, and of employing the usual means of conveyance. But it is denied that the government has its choice of means; or, that it may employ the most convenient means, if, to employ them, it be necessary to erect a corporation.

On what foundation does this argument rest? On this alone: The power of creating a corporation, is one appertaining to sovereignty, and is not expressly conferred on Congress. This is true. But all legislative powers appertain to sovereignty. The original power of giving the law on any subject whatever, is a sovereign power; and if the government of the Union is restrained from creating a corporation, as a means for performing its functions, on the single reason that the creation of a corporation is an act of sovereignty; if the sufficiency of this reason be acknowledged, there would be some difficulty in sustaining the authority of Congress to pass other laws for the accomplishment of the same objects.

The government which has a right to do an act, and has imposed on it the duty of performing that act, must, according to the dictates of reason, be allowed to select the means; and those who contend that it may not select any appropriate means, that one particular mode of effecting the object is excepted, take upon themselves the burden of establishing that exception.

The creation of a corporation, it is said, appertains to sovereignty. This is admitted. But to what portion of sovereignty does it appertain? Does it belong to one more than to another? In America, the powers of sovereignty are divided between the government of the Union, and those of the States. They are each sovereign, with respect to the objects committed to it, and neither sovereign with respect to the objects committed to the other. . . . The power of creating a corporation, though appertaining to sovereignty, is not, like the power of making war, or levying taxes, or of regulating commerce, a great substantive and independent power, which cannot be implied as incidental to other powers, or used as a means of executing them. It is never the end for which other powers are exercised, but a means by which other objects are accomplished. No contributions are made to charity for the sake of an incorporation, but a corporation is created to administer the charity; no seminary of learning is instituted in order to be incorporated, but the corporate character is conferred to subserve the purposes of education. No city was ever built with the sole object of being incorporated, but is incorporated as affording the best means of being well governed. The power of creating a corporation is never used for its own sake, but for the purpose of effecting something else. No sufficient reason is, therefore, perceived, why it may not pass as incidental to those powers which are expressly given, if it be a direct mode of executing them.

But the constitution of the United States has not left the right of Congress to employ the necessary means for the execution of the powers conferred on the government to general reasoning. To its enumeration of powers is added that of making "all laws which shall be necessary and proper, for carrying into execution the foregoing powers, and all other powers vested by this constitution, in the government of the United States, or in any department thereof."

.... A government is created by the people, having legislative, executive, and judicial powers. Its legislative powers are vested in a Congress, which is to consist of a senate and house of representatives. Each house may determine the rule of its proceedings; and it is declared that every bill which shall have passed both houses, shall, before it becomes a law, be presented to the President of the United States. The seventh section describes the course of proceedings, by which a bill shall become a law; and, then the eighth section enumerates the powers of Congress. Could it be necessary to say that a legislature should exercise legislative powers in the shape of legislation? After allowing each house to prescribe its own course of proceeding, after describing the manner in which a bill should become a law, would it have entered into the mind of a single member of the convention that an express power to make laws was necessary to enable the legislature to make them? That a legislature, endowed with legislative powers, can legislate, is a proposition too self-evident to have been questioned.

.... To employ the means necessary to an end, is generally understood as employing any means calculated to produce the end, and not as being confined to those single means, without which the end would be entirely unattainable. Such is the character of human language, that no word conveys to the mind, in all situations, one single definite idea: and nothing is more common than to use words in a figurative sense. . . .

[I]n the case under consideration[, t]he subject is the execution of those great powers on which the welfare of a nation essentially depends. It must have been the intention of those who gave these powers, to insure, as far as human prudence could insure, their beneficial execution.

This could not be done by confiding the choice of means to such narrow limits as not to leave it in the power of Congress to adopt any which might be appropriate, and which were conducive to the end. This provision is made in a constitution intended to endure for ages to come, and, consequently, to be adapted to the various crises of human affairs. To have prescribed the means by which government should, in all future time, execute its powers, would have been to change, entirely, the character of the instrument, and give it the properties of a legal code. It would have been an unwise attempt to provide, by immutable rules, for exigencies which, if foreseen at all, must have been seen dimly, and which can be best provided for as they occur. To have declared that the best means shall not be used, but those alone without which the power given would be nugatory, would have been to deprive the legislature of the capacity to avail itself of experience, to exercise its reason, and to accommodate its legislation to circumstances. If we apply this principle of construction to any of the powers of the government, we shall find it so pernicious in its operation that we shall be compelled to discard it. The powers vested in Congress may certainly be carried into execution, without prescribing an oath of office. The power to exact this security for the faithful performance of duty, is not given, nor is it indispensably necessary. The different departments may be established; taxes may be imposed and collected; armies and navies may be raised and maintained; and money may be borrowed, without requiring an oath of office. It might be argued, with as much plausibility as other incidental powers have been assailed, that the convention was not unmindful of this subject. The oath which might be exacted - that of fidelity to the constitution - is prescribed, and no other can be required. Yet, he would be charged with insanity who should contend that the legislature might not superadd, to the oath directed by the constitution, such other oath of office as its wisdom might suggest.

So, with respect to the whole penal code of the United States: whence arises the power to punish in cases not prescribed by the constitution? All admit that the government may, legitimately, punish any violation of its laws; and yet, this is not among the enumerated powers of Congress. The right to enforce the observance of law, by punishing its infraction, might be denied with the more plausibility because it is expressly given in some cases. . . .

The baneful influence of this narrow construction on all the operations of the government, and the absolute impracticability of maintaining it without rendering the government incompetent to its great objects, might be illustrated by numerous examples drawn from the constitution, and from our laws. The good sense of the public has pronounced, without hesitation, that the power of punishment appertains to sovereignty, and may be exercised whenever the sovereign has a right to act, as incidental to his constitutional powers. It is a means for carrying into execution all sovereign powers, and may be used, although not indispensably necessary. It is a right incidental to the power, and conducive to its beneficial exercise.

. . . . We admit, as all must admit, that the powers of the government are limited, and that its limits are not to be transcended. But we think the sound construction of the constitution must allow to the national legislature that discretion, with respect to the means by which the powers it confers are to be carried into execution, which will enable that body to perform the high duties assigned to it, in the manner most beneficial to the people. Let the end be legitimate, let it be within the scope of the constitution, and all means which are appropriate, which are plainly adapted to that end, which are not prohibited, but consist with the letter and spirit of the constitution, are constitutional.

That a corporation must be considered as a means not less usual, not of higher dignity, not more requiring a particular specification than other means, has been sufficiently proved. If we look to the origin of corporations, to the manner in which they have been framed in that government from which we have derived most of our legal principles and ideas, or to the uses to which they have been applied, we find no reason to suppose that a constitution, omitting, and wisely omitting, to enumerate all the means for carrying into execution the great powers vested in government, ought to have specified this. Had it been intended to grant this power as one which should be distinct and independent, to be exercised in any case whatever, it would have found a place among the enumerated powers of the government. But being considered merely as a means, to be employed only for the purpose of carrying into execution the given powers, there could be no motive for particularly mentioning it.

. . . . If a corporation may be employed indiscriminately with other means to carry into execution the powers of the government, no particular reason can be assigned for excluding the use of a bank, if required for its fiscal operations. To use one, must be within the discretion of Congress, if it be an appropriate mode of executing the powers of government. . . .

Should Congress, in the execution of its powers, adopt measures which are prohibited by the constitution; or should Congress, under the pretext of executing its powers, pass laws for the accomplishment of objects not entrusted to the government, it would become the painful duty of this tribunal, should a case requiring such a decision come before it, to say that such an act was not the law of the land. But where the law is not prohibited, and is really calculated to effect any of the objects entrusted to the government, to undertake here to inquire into the degree of its necessity, would be to pass the line which circumscribes the judicial department, and to tread on legislative ground. This court disclaims all pretensions to such a power.

After this declaration, it can scarcely be necessary to say that the existence of state banks can have no possible influence on the question. No trace is to be found in the constitution of an intention to create a dependence of the government of the Union on those of the states, for the execution of the great powers assigned to it. Its means are adequate to its ends; and on those means alone was it expected to rely for the accomplishment of its ends. To impose on it the necessity of resorting to means which it cannot control, which another government may furnish or withhold, would render its course precarious; the result of its measures uncertain, and create a dependence on other governments, which might disappoint its most important designs, and is incompatible with the language of the constitution. But were it otherwise, the choice of means implies a right to choose a national bank in preference to state banks, and Congress alone can make the election.

After the most deliberate consideration, it is the unanimous and decided opinion of this court that the act to incorporate the [Second B]ank of the United States is a law made in pursuance of the constitution, and is a part of the supreme law of the land.

The branches, proceeding from the same stock, and being conducive to the complete accomplishment of the object, are equally constitutional. It would have been unwise to locate them in the charter, and it would be unnecessarily inconvenient to employ the legislative power in making those subordinate arrangements. The great duties of the bank are prescribed; those duties require branches; and the bank itself may, we think, be safely trusted with the selection of places where those branches shall be fixed; reserving always to the government the right to require that a branch shall be located where it may be deemed necessary.

It being the opinion of the court that the act incorporating the bank is constitutional, and that the power of establishing a branch in the state of Maryland might be properly exercised by the bank itself, we proceed to inquire:

Whether the state of Maryland may, without violating the constitution, tax that branch?

That the power of taxation is one of vital importance; that it is retained by the states; that it is not abridged by the grant of a similar power to the government of the Union; that it is to be concurrently exercised by the two governments; are truths which have never been denied. But, such is the paramount character of the constitution that its capacity to withdraw any subject from the action of even this power, is admitted. The states are expressly forbidden to lay any duties on imports or exports, except what may be absolutely necessary for executing their inspection laws. If the obligation of this prohibition must be conceded - if it may restrain a state from the exercise of its taxing power on imports and exports - the same paramount character would seem to restrain, as it certainly may restrain, a state from such other exercise of this power, as is in its nature incompatible with, and repugnant to, the constitutional laws of the Union. A law, absolutely repugnant to another, as entirely repeals that other as if express terms of repeal were used.

. . . . [T]he constitution and the laws made in pursuance thereof are supreme; . . . they control the constitution and laws of the respective states, and cannot be controlled by them. . . . [A] power to create implies a power to preserve. . . . [A] power to destroy, if wielded by a different hand, is hostile to, and incompatible with these powers to create and to preserve. . . . [W]here this repugnancy exists, that authority which is supreme must control, not yield to that over which it is supreme.

These propositions, as abstract truths, would, perhaps, never be controverted. Their application to this case, however, has been denied; and, both in maintaining the affirmative and the negative, a splendor of eloquence, and strength of argument seldom, if ever, surpassed, have been displayed.

. . . . That the power of taxing [the bank] by the states may be exercised so as to destroy it, is too obvious to be denied. But taxation is said to be an absolute power, which acknowledges no other limits than those expressly prescribed in the constitution, and like sovereign power of every other description, is trusted to the discretion of those who use it. But the very terms of this argument admit that the sovereignty of the state, in the article of taxation itself, is subordinate to, and may be controlled by the constitution of the United States. How far it has been controlled by that instrument must be a question of construction. In making this construction, no principle not declared can be admissible, which would defeat the legitimate operations of a supreme government. It is of the very essence of supremacy to remove all obstacles to its action within its own sphere, and so to modify every power vested in subordinate governments as to exempt its own operations from their own influence. . . .

It is admitted that the power of taxing the people and their property is essential to the very existence of government, and may be legitimately exercised on the objects to which it is applicable, to the utmost extent to which the government may choose to carry it. The only security against the abuse of this power is found in the structure of the government itself. In imposing a tax the legislature acts upon its constituents. This is in general a sufficient security against erroneous and oppressive taxation.

The people of a state, therefore, give to their government a right of taxing themselves and their property, and as the exigencies of government cannot be limited, they prescribe no limits to the exercise of this right, resting confidently on the interest of the legislator, and on the influence of the constituents over their representative, to guard them against its abuse. But the means employed by the government of the Union have no such security, nor is the right of a state to tax them sustained by the same theory. Those means are not given by the people of a particular state, not given by the constituents of the legislature, which claim the right to tax them, but by the people of all the states. They are given by all, for the benefit of all - and upon theory, should be subjected to that government only which belongs to all.

. . . . All subjects over which the sovereign power of a state extends, are objects of taxation; but those over which it does not extend, are, upon the soundest principles, exempt from taxation. This proposition may almost be pronounced self-evident.

The sovereignty of a state extends to everything which exists by its own authority, or is introduced by its permission; but does it extend to those means which are employed by Congress to carry into execution - powers conferred on that body by the people of the United States? We think it demonstrable that it does not. Those powers are not given by the people of a single state. They are given by the people of the United States, to a government whose laws, made in pursuance of the constitution, are declared to be supreme. Consequently, the people of a single state cannot confer a sovereignty which will extend over them.

If we measure the power of taxation residing in a state, by the extent of sovereignty which the people of a single state possess, and can confer on its government, we have an intelligible standard, applicable to every case to which the power may be applied. We have a principle which leaves the power of taxing the people and property of a state unimpaired; which leaves to a state the command of all its resources, and which places beyond its reach, all those powers which are conferred by the people of the United States on the government of the Union, and all those means which are given for the purpose of carrying those powers into execution. We have a principle which is safe for the states, and safe for the Union. We are relieved, as we ought to be, from clashing sovereignty; from interfering powers; from a repugnancy between a right in one government to pull down what there is an acknowledged right in another to build up; from the incompatibility of a right in one government to destroy what there is a right in another to preserve. We are not driven to the perplexing inquiry, so unfit for the judicial department, what degree of taxation is the legitimate use, and what degree may amount to the abuse of the power. The attempt to use it on the means employed by the government of the Union, in pursuance of the constitution, is itself an abuse, because it is the usurpation of a power which the people of a single state cannot give.

We find, then, on just theory, a total failure of this original right to tax the means employed by the government of the Union, for the execution of its powers. The right never existed, and the question whether it has been surrendered, cannot arise.

. . . . That the power to tax involves the power to destroy; that the power to destroy may defeat and render useless the power to create; that there is a plain repugnance, in conferring on one government a power to control the constitutional measures of another, which other, with respect to those very measures, is declared to be supreme over that which exerts the control, are propositions not to be denied. . . .

If the states may tax one instrument, employed by the government in the execution of its powers, they may tax any and every other instrument. They may tax the mail; they may tax the mint; they may tax patent-rights; they may tax the papers of the custom-house; they may tax judicial process; they may tax all the means employed by the government, to an excess which would defeat all the ends of government. This was not intended by the American people. They did not design to make their government dependent on the states.

. . . . If the controlling power of the states be established; if their supremacy as to taxation be acknowledged; what is to restrain their exercising this control in any shape they may please to give it? Their sovereignty is not confined to taxation. That is not the only mode in which it might be displayed. The question is, in truth, a question of supremacy; and if the right of the states to tax the means employed by the general government be conceded, the declaration that the constitution, and the laws made in pursuance thereof, shall be the supreme law of the land, is empty and unmeaning declamation.

. . . . [W]hen a state taxes the operations of the government of the United States, it acts upon institutions created, not by their own constituents, but by people over whom they claim no control. It acts upon the measures of a government created by others as well as themselves, for the benefit of others in common with themselves. The difference is that which always exists, and always must exist, between the action of the whole on a part, and the action of a part on the whole - between the laws of a government declared to be supreme, and those of a government which, when in opposition to those laws, is not supreme.

But if the full application of this argument could be admitted, it might bring into question the right of Congress to tax the state banks, and could not prove the right of the states to tax the Bank of the United States.

The court has bestowed on this subject its most deliberate consideration. The result is a conviction that the states have no power, by taxation or otherwise, to retard, impede, burden, or in any manner control the operations of the constitutional laws enacted by Congress to carry into

execution the powers vested in the general government.
This is, we think, the unavoidable consequence of that supremacy which the constitution has declared.

We are unanimously of opinion that the law passed by the
legislature of Maryland, imposing a tax on the Bank of
the United States, is unconstitutional and void.

This opinion does not deprive the states of any resources
which they originally possessed. It does not extend to a
tax paid by the real property of the bank, in common with
the other real property within the state, nor to a tax imposed on the interest which the citizens of Maryland may
hold in this institution, in common with other property of
the same description throughout the state. But this is a
tax on the operations of the bank, and is, consequently, a
tax on the operation of an instrument employed by the
government of the Union to carry its powers into execution. Such a tax must be unconstitutional.

Chief Justice Marshall's landmark decision in McCulloch
v. Maryland *established that the Supremacy Clause protected federal laws from state interference. It did not protect
The Second Bank of the United States from Andrew Jackson. In 1832 The Bank asked Congress for an extension of
its charter. On July 10, after Congress voted for the extension, President Jackson, a vehement opponent of the Bank,
vetoed it. Jackson, in a veto message written partially by
his Attorney General [and future Chief Justice] Roger
Brooke Taney said: "The opinion of the judges has no more
authority over Congress, than the opinion of Congress has
over the judges, and on that point the President is independent of both. . . . Many of our rich men have not been
content with equal protection and equal benefits but have
besought us to make them richer by an act of Congress."*

THE TRAIL OF TEARS
The Cherokee Nation v. Georgia

From time immemorial the Cherokee Nation have composed a sovereign and independent State, and in this character have been repeatedly recognized by the United States, in various treaties subsisting between their nation and the United States.

John Ross, Chief of the Cherokee Nation
December 27, 1830

From time immemorial a part of the Cherokee Nation lived between the Savannah and Altamaha rivers in what is now Georgia. The Cherokee Nation sought protection from white settlers by signing treaties with the United States (the Hopewell Treaty in 1785 and the Holston Treaty in 1791), in which the Nation was recognized as a sovereign and independent state under the protection of the United States. The Cherokees were guaranteed by these, and other treaties, and by an Act of Congress dated March 30, 1802, the right to self-government without interference from any State or the United States.

In the late 1820's gold was discovered on Cherokee lands. On December 12, 1829 Georgia passed a law entitled "An Act to add the Territory of the Cherokee Indians to Carroll, DeKalb, Gwinett, Hall and Habersham Counties." The law seized all Cherokee lands; abolished all Cherokee laws and ended the Cherokee Nation's political existence. The Georgia militia was to enforce the law.

When President Andrew Jackson refused to honor the U.S. Government's treaty obligation to protect the Cherokee Nation, they petitioned the United States Supreme Court to protect them from the State of Georgia.

On March 18, 1831 Chief Justice John Marshall announced the 5-2 decision of the Court. The edited text follows.

THE CHEROKEE NATION COURT

Chief Justice John Marshall
Appointed by President John Adams
Served 1801 - 1835

Associate Justice William Johnson
Appointed by President Jefferson
Served 1804 - 1834

Associate Justice Joseph Story
Appointed by President Madison
Served 1811 - 1845

Associate Justice Gabriel Duvall
Appointed by President Madison
Served 1811 - 1835

Associate Justice Smith Thompson
Appointed by President Monroe
Served 1823 - 1843

Associate Justice John McLean
Appointed by President Van Buren
Served 1829 - 1861

Associate Justice Henry Baldwin
Appointed by President Jackson
Served 1830 - 1844

The unedited text of *The Cherokee Nation v. Georgia* can be found on page 1, volume 30 of *United States Reports.*

THE CHEROKEE NATION v. GEORGIA
MARCH 18, 1831

CHIEF JUSTICE MARSHALL: This bill is brought by the Cherokee Nation, praying an injunction [court order to stop an action] to restrain the State of Georgia from the execution of certain laws of that State, which, as is alleged, go directly to annihilate the Cherokees as a political society, and to seize, for the use of Georgia, the lands of the nation which have been assured to them by the United States in solemn treaties repeatedly made and still in force.

If courts were permitted to indulge their sympathies, a case better calculated to excite them can scarcely be imagined. A people once numerous, powerful, and truly independent, found by our ancestors in the quiet and uncontrolled possession of an ample domain, gradually sinking beneath our superior policy, our arts and our arms, have yielded their lands by successive treaties, each of which contains a solemn guarantee of the residue, until they retain no more of their formerly extensive territory than is deemed necessary to their comfortable subsistence. To preserve this remnant the present application is made.

Before we can look into the merits of the case, a preliminary inquiry presents itself. Has this court jurisdiction of the cause?

The third article of the Constitution describes the extent of the judicial power. The second section closes an enumeration of the cases to which it is extended, with "controversies" "between a State or the citizens thereof, and foreign states, citizens, or subjects." A subsequent clause of the same section gives the Supreme Court origi-

nal jurisdiction in all cases in which a State shall be a party. The party defendant [Georgia] may then unquestionably be sued in this court. May the plaintiff [Cherokee
Nation] sue in it? Is the Cherokee Nation a foreign state
in the sense in which that term is used in the Constitution?

The counsel for the [Cherokee Nation] have maintained
the affirmative of this proposition with great earnestness
and ability. So much of the argument as was intended to
prove the character of the Cherokees as a State, as a distinct political society separated from others, capable of
managing its own affairs and governing itself, has, in the
opinion of a majority of the judges, been completely successful. They have been uniformly treated as a State
from the settlement of our country. The numerous
treaties made with them by the United States recognize
them as a people capable of maintaining the relations of
peace and war, of being responsible in their political character for any violation of their engagements, or for any
aggression committed on the citizens of the United States
by any individual of their community. Laws have been
enacted in the spirit of these treaties. The acts of our
government plainly recognize the Cherokee Nation as a
State, and the courts are bound by those acts.

A question of much more difficulty remains. Do the
Cherokees constitute a foreign state in the sense of the
Constitution?

The counsel have shown conclusively that they are not a
State of the Union, and have insisted that individually
they are aliens, not owing allegiance to the United States.

An aggregate of aliens composing a State must, they say, be a foreign state. Each individual being foreign, the whole must be foreign.

This argument is imposing, but we must examine it more closely before we yield to it. The condition of the Indians in relation to the United States is perhaps unlike that of any other two people in existence. In the general, nations not owing a common allegiance are foreign to each other. The term *foreign nation* is, with strict propriety, applicable by either to the other. But the relation of the Indians to the United States is marked by peculiar and cardinal distinctions which exist nowhere else.

The Indian Territory is admitted to compose a part of the United States. In all our maps, geographical treaties, histories and laws, it is so considered. In all our intercourse with foreign nations, in our commercial regulations, in any attempt at intercourse between Indians and foreign nations, they are considered as within the jurisdictional limits of the United States, subject to many of those restraints which are imposed upon our own citizens. They acknowledge themselves in their treaties to be under the protection of the United States; they admit that the United States shall have the sole and exclusive right of regulating the trade with them, and managing all their affairs as they think proper; and the Cherokees in particular were allowed by the treaty of Hopewell, which preceded the Constitution, "to send a deputy of their choice, whenever they think fit, to Congress." Treaties were made with some tribes by the State of New York under a then unsettled construction of the confederation, by which they ceded all their lands to that State, taking back a limited grant to themselves, in which they admit their dependence.

Though the Indians are acknowledged to have an unques-
tionable, and, heretofore, unquestioned right to the lands
they occupy until that right shall be extinguished by a
voluntary cession to our government, yet it may well be
doubted whether those tribes which reside within the acknowledged boundaries of the United States can, with
strict accuracy, be denominated foreign nations. They
may, more correctly, perhaps, be denominated domestic
dependent nations. They occupy a territory to which we
assert a title independent of their will, which must take
effect in point of possession when their right of possession ceases. Meanwhile they are in a state of pupilage.
Their relation to the United States resembles that of a
ward to his guardian.

They look to our government for protection; rely upon its
kindness and its power; appeal to it for relief to their
wants; and address the President as their great father.
They and their country are considered by foreign nations,
as well as by ourselves, as being so completely under the
sovereignty and dominion of the United States, that any
attempt to acquire their lands, or to form a political connection with them, would be considered by all as an invasion of our territory, and an act of hostility.

These considerations go far to support the opinion that
the framers of our Constitution had not the Indian tribes
in view when they opened the courts of the Union to controversies between a State or the citizens thereof, and foreign states.

In considering this subject, the habits and usages of the
Indians in their intercourse with their white neighbors
ought not to be entirely disregarded. At the time the Constitution was framed, the idea of appealing to an Ameri-

can court of justice for an assertion of right or a redress
of wrong, had perhaps never entered the mind of an Indian or of his tribe. Their appeal was to the tomahawk,
[not] to the government. This was well understood by the
statesmen who framed the Constitution of the United
States, and might furnish some reason for omitting to enumerate them among the parties who might sue in the
courts of the Union. Be this as it may, the peculiar relations between the United States and the Indians occupying
our territory are such that we should feel much difficulty
in considering them as designated by the term *foreign
State*, were there no other part of the Constitution which
might shed light on the meaning of these words. But we
think that in construing [interpreting] them, considerable
aid is furnished by that clause in the eighth section of the
third article, which empowers Congress to "regulate commerce with foreign nations, and among the several States,
and with the Indian tribes."

In this clause they are as clearly contradistinguished by a
name appropriate to themselves from foreign nations as
from the several States composing the Union. They are
designated by a distinct appellation; and as this appellation can be applied to neither of the others, neither can
the appellation distinguishing either of the others be in
fair construction applied to them. The objects to which
the power of regulating commerce might be directed, are
divided into three distinct classes - foreign nations, the
several States, and Indian tribes. When forming this article, the convention considered them as entirely distinct.
We cannot assume that the distinction was lost in framing
a subsequent article, unless there be something in its language to authorize the assumption.

The counsel for the plaintiffs [Cherokee Nation] contend
that the words "Indian tribes" were introduced into the article empowering Congress to regulate commerce for the
purpose of removing those doubts in which the management of Indian affairs was involved by the language of
the ninth article of the confederation. Intending to give
the whole power of managing those affairs to the government about to be instituted, the convention conferred it
explicitly; and omitted those qualifications which embar-
rassed the exercise of it as granted in the confederation.
This may be admitted without weakening the construction
which has been intimated. Had the Indian tribes been foreign nations, in the view of the convention, this exclusive
power of regulating intercourse with them might have
been, and most probably would have been, specifically
given in language indicating that idea, not in language
contradistinguishing them from foreign nations. Congress
might have been empowered "to regulate commerce with
foreign nations, including the Indian tribes, and among
the several States." This language would have suggested
itself to statesmen who considered the Indian tribes as foreign nations, and were yet desirous of mentioning them
particularly.

It has been also said that the same words have not necessarily the same meaning attached to them when found in
different parts of the same instrument: their meaning is
controlled by the context. This is undoubtedly true. In
common language the same word has various meanings,
and the peculiar sense in which it is used in any sentence
is to be determined by the context. This may not be
equally true with respect to proper names. Foreign nations is a general term, the application of which to Indian
tribes, when used in the American Constitution, is at best
extremely questionable. In one article in which a power is

given to be exercised in regard to foreign nations generally, and to the Indian tribes particularly, they are mentioned as separate in terms clearly contradistinguishing
them from each other. We perceive plainly that the Constitution in this article does not comprehend Indian tribes
in the general term "foreign nations;" not, we presume, because a tribe may not be a nation, but because it is not
foreign to the United States. When, afterwards, the term
"foreign State" is introduced, we cannot impute to the
convention the intention to desert its former meaning, and
to comprehend Indian tribes within it, unless the context
force that construction on us. We find nothing in the
context, and nothing in the subject of the article, which
leads to it.

The court has bestowed its best attention on this question,
and, after mature deliberation, the majority is of opinion
that an Indian tribe or nation within the United States is
not a foreign state in the sense of the Constitution, and
cannot maintain an action in the courts of the United
States.

A serious additional objection exists to the jurisdiction of
the court. Is the matter of the bill the proper subject for
judicial inquiry and decision? It seeks to restrain a State
from the forcible exercise of legislative power over a
neighboring people asserting their independence, their
right to which the State denies. On several of the matters
alleged in the bill, for example on the laws making it
criminal to exercise the usual powers of self-government
in their own country by the Cherokee Nation, this court
cannot interpose, at least in the form in which those matters are presented.

That part of the bill which respects the land occupied by the Indians and prays the aid of the court to protect their possession, may be more doubtful. The mere question of right might perhaps be decided by this court in a proper case with proper parties. But the court is asked to do more than decide on the title. The bill requires us to control the Legislature of Georgia, and to restrain the exertion of its physical force. The propriety of such an interposition by the court may be well questioned. It savors too much of the exercise of political power to be within the proper province of the judicial department. But the opinion on the point respecting parties makes it unnecessary to decide this question.

If it be true that the Cherokee Nation have rights, this is not the tribunal in which those rights are to be asserted. If it be true that wrongs have been inflicted, and that still greater are to be apprehended, this is not the tribunal which can redress the past or prevent the future.

The motion for an injunction is denied.

In The Cherokee Nation v. Georgia *the Supreme Court refused to rule on the legality of the Georgia Acts and the status of the Cherokee Treaties, finding that the Cherokees, a "domestic dependent nation," could not bring suit in Federal Court.*

The following year an American citizen, Samuel Worcester, brought the legality of the Georgia Acts and the status of the Cherokee Treaties back to the Court for a final determination.

THE TRAIL OF TEARS

Worcester v. Georgia

All white persons residing within the limits of the Chero-
kee Nation on the 1st day of March next, or anytime
thereafter, without permission of the Governor shall be
guilty of a high misdemeanor and shall be punished by
confinement in the penitentiary at hard labor.

An Act of Georgia, December 22, 1830

On December 22, 1830 Georgia passed a law entitled, "An
Act to prevent white persons from residing within that
part of Georgia occupied by the Cherokee Indians."

Samuel Worcester, a missionary, residing within the
Cherokee Nation, with the permission of the Cherokees,
but without the permission of the Governor of Georgia,
was arrested in July 1831 for violating the December
22nd Act. He was tried in the Gwinnett County Superior
Court, found guilty, and sentenced to four years' hard labor. Worcester appealed to the Supreme Court. He asserted that Georgia had no jurisdiction within the Cherokee Nation and that their Acts of December 12, 1829 (in
which they claimed jurisdiction) and December 22, 1830
(on which he had been convicted) were in violation of the
treaties still in force between the United States and the
Cherokee Nation. Worcester brought back before the Supreme Court the issues they had refused to rule on the
previous year in *The Cherokee Nation v. Georgia*. The
Supreme Court's refusal had been based on the grounds
that the Cherokees were a "domestic dependent nation"
with no right to file suit in a U.S. Court. Samuel Worcester, a citizen of Vermont, had no such restriction.

On March 3, 1832 Chief Justice John Marshall announced
the 6-1 decision of the Court. The edited text follows.

THE WORCESTER COURT

Chief Justice John Marshall
Appointed by President John Adams
Served 1801 - 1835

Associate Justice William Johnson
Appointed by President Jefferson
Served 1804 - 1834

Associate Justice Joseph Story
Appointed by President Madison
Served 1811 - 1845

Associate Justice Gabriel Duvall
Appointed by President Madison
Served 1811 - 1835

Associate Justice Smith Thompson
Appointed by President Monroe
Served 1823 - 1843

Associate Justice John McLean
Appointed by President Van Buren
Served 1829 - 1861

Associate Justice Henry Baldwin
Appointed by President Jackson
Served 1830 - 1844

The unedited text of *Worcester v. Georgia* can be found
on page 515, volume 31 of *United States Reports.*

WORCESTER v. GEORGIA
MARCH 2, 1832

CHIEF JUSTICE MARSHALL: This cause, in every point of view in which it can be placed, is of the deepest interest.

The defendant [Georgia] is a State, a member of the Union, which has exercised the powers of government over a people who deny its jurisdiction, and are under the protection of the United States.

The plaintiff [Worcester] is a citizen of the State of Vermont, condemned to hard labor for four years in the penitentiary of Georgia, under color of an act which he alleges to be repugnant to the Constitution, laws, and treaties of the United States.

The legislative power of a State, the controlling power of the Constitution and laws of the United States, the rights, if they have any, the political existence of a once numerous and powerful people, the personal liberty of a citizen, are all involved in the subject now to be considered.

. . . . The indictment charges the plaintiff [Worcester] and others, being white persons, with the offense of "residing within the limits of the Cherokee Nation without a license," and "without having taken the oath to support and defend the constitution and laws of the State of Georgia."

[Worcester] filed the following plea [in the state court]:

"And the said Samuel A. Worcester, in his own proper person, comes and says that this court ought not to take further cognizance of the action and prosecution aforesaid, because, he says, that on the 15th day of July, in the year 1831, he was, and still is, a resident in the Cherokee Nation; and that the said supposed crime or crimes, and each of them, were committed, if committed at all, at the town of New Echota, in the said Cherokee Nation, out of the jurisdiction of this court, and not in the County Gwinnett, or elsewhere, within the jurisdiction of this court; and this defendant saith that he is a citizen of the State of Vermont, one of the United States of America, and that he entered the aforesaid Cherokee Nation in the capacity of a duly authorized missionary of the American Board of Commissioners for Foreign Missions, under the authority of the President of the United States, and has not since been required by him to leave it; that he was, at the time of his arrest, engaged in preaching the Gospel to the Cherokee Indians, and in translating the sacred Scriptures into their language, with the permission and approval of the said Cherokee Nation, and in accordance with the humane policy of the government of the United States for the civilization and improvement of the Indians; and that his residence there, for this purpose, is the residence charged in the aforesaid indictment; and this defendant further saith that this prosecution the State of Georgia ought not to have or maintain, because, he saith, that several treaties have, from time to time, been entered into between the United States and the Cherokee Nation of Indians [between November 1785 and February 1819], all which treaties have been duly ratified by the Senate of the United States of

America, and by which treaties the United States
of America acknowledge the said Cherokee Nation to be a sovereign nation, authorized to govern themselves, and all persons who have settled
within their territory, free from any right of legislative interference by the several States composing the United States of America, in reference to
acts done within their own territory; and by
which treaties the whole of the territory now occupied by the Cherokee Nation on the east of the
Mississippi has been solemnly guaranteed to
them; all of which treaties are existing treaties at
this day, and in full force.

"By these treaties . . . the aforesaid territory is acknowledged to lie without the jurisdiction of the
several States composing the Union of the United
States; and it is thereby specially stipulated that
the citizens of the United States shall not enter
the aforesaid territory, even on a visit, without a
passport from the governor of a State, or from
some one duly authorized thereto by the President of the United States; all of which will more
fully and at large appear by reference to the
aforesaid treaties. And this defendant saith, that
the several acts charged in the bill of indictment
were done, or omitted to be done, if at all, within
the said territory so recognized as belonging to
the said nation, and so, as aforesaid, held by them,
under the guarantee of the United States; that,
for those acts, the defendant is not amenable to
the laws of Georgia, nor to the jurisdiction of the
courts of the said State: and that the laws of the
State of Georgia, which profess to add the said
territory to the several adjacent counties of the

said State, and to extend the laws of Georgia over the said territory and persons inhabiting the same; and, in particular, the act on which this indictment against this defendant is grounded, to wit, 'An Act entitled an Act to prevent the exercise of assumed and arbitrary power by all persons under pretext of authority from the Cherokee Indians, and their laws, and to prevent white persons from residing within that part of the chartered limits of Georgia occupied by the Cherokee Indians, and to provide a guard for the protection of the gold mines, and to enforce the laws of the State within the aforesaid territory,' are repugnant to the aforesaid treaties; which, according to the Constitution of the United States, compose a part of the supreme law of the land; and that these laws of Georgia are, therefore, unconstitutional, void, and of no effect; that the said laws of Georgia are also unconstitutional and void, because they impair the obligation of the various contracts formed by and between the aforesaid Cherokee Nation and the said United States of America, as above recited; also, that the said laws of Georgia are unconstitutional and void, because they interfere with, and attempt to regulate and control the intercourse with the said Cherokee Nation, which, by the said Constitution, belongs exclusively to the Congress of the United States; and because the said laws are repugnant to the statute of the United States, passed [in] March, 1802, entitled 'An Act to regulate trade and intercourse with the Indian tribes, and to preserve peace on the frontier;' and that, therefore, this court has no jurisdiction to cause this defendant to make further or other answer to the said

bill of indictment, or further to try and punish
this defendant for the said supposed offense or
offenses alleged in the bill of indictment, or any
of them; and, therefore, this defendant prays
[asks] judgment whether he shall be held bound
to answer further to said indictment."

This plea was overruled by the court, and the prisoner, being arraigned [charged with an offense], pleaded not
guilty. The jury found a verdict against him, and the
court sentenced him to hard labor in the penitentiary for
the term of four years.

. . . . It is, . . . we think, too clear for controversy, that the
act of Congress by which this court is constituted, has giv-
en it the power, and of course imposed on it the duty, of
exercising jurisdiction in this case. This duty, however
unpleasant, cannot be avoided. Those who fill the judicial
department have no discretion in selecting the subjects to
be brought before them. We must examine the defense
set up in this plea. We must inquire and decide whether
the act of the Legislature of Georgia under which
[Worcester] has been prosecuted and condemned, be consistent with, or repugnant to the Constitution, laws and
treaties of the United States.

. . . . [T]he particular statute and section on which the indictment is founded . . . enacts that "all white persons, residing within the limits of the Cherokee Nation on the 1st
day of March next, or at any time thereafter, without a license or permit from his excellency the governor, or from
such agent as his excellency the governor shall authorize
to grant such permit or license, and who shall not have
taken the oath hereinafter required, shall be guilty of a
high misdemeanor, and, upon conviction thereof, shall be

punished by confinement to the penitentiary, at hard labor for a term not less than four years."

The eleventh section authorizes the governor, should he deem it necessary for the protection of the mines, or the enforcement of the laws in force within the Cherokee Nation, to raise and organize a guard, etc.

The thirteenth section enacts, "that the said guard or any member of them, shall be, and they are hereby authorized and empowered to arrest any person legally charged with or detected in a violation of the laws of this State, and to convey, as soon as practicable, the person so arrested, before a justice of the peace, judge of the superior, or justice of inferior court of this State, to be dealt with according to law."

The extraterritorial power of every Legislature being limited in its action to its own citizens or subjects, the very passage of this act is an assertion of jurisdiction over the Cherokee Nation. . . .

The first step, then, in the inquiry which the Constitution and laws impose on this court, is an examination of the rightfulness of this claim.

America, separated from Europe by a wide ocean, was inhabited by a distinct people, divided into separate nations, independent of each other and of the rest of the world, having institutions of their own, and governing themselves by their own laws.   It is difficult to comprehend the proposition that the inhabitants of either quarter of the globe could have rightful original claims of dominion over the inhabitants of the other, or over the lands they occupied; or that the discovery of either by the other should give the discoverer rights in the country discovered which annulled the pre-existing rights of its ancient possessors.

After lying concealed for a series of ages, the enterprise of Europe, guided by nautical science, conducted some of her adventurous sons into this western world. They found it in possession of a people who had made small progress in agriculture or manufactures, and whose general employment was war, hunting, and fishing.

Did these adventurers, by sailing along the coast and occasionally landing on it, acquire for the several governments to whom they belonged, or by whom they were commissioned, a rightful property in the soil from the Atlantic to the Pacific; or rightful dominion over the numerous people who occupied it? Or has nature, or the great Creator of all things, conferred these rights over hunters and fishermen, on agriculturists and manufacturers?

But power, war, conquest, give rights, which, after possession, are conceded by the world; and which can never be controverted by those on whom they descend. We proceed, then, to the actual state of things, having glanced at their origin, because holding it in our recollection might shed some light on existing pretensions.

The great maritime powers of Europe discovered and visited different parts of this continent at nearly the same time. The object was too immense for any one of them to grasp the whole, and the claimants were too powerful to submit to the exclusive or unreasonable pretensions of any single potentate. To avoid bloody conflicts, which might terminate disastrously to all, it was necessary for the nations of Europe to establish some principle which

all would acknowledge, and which should decide their respective rights as between themselves. This principle, suggested by the actual state of things, was, "That discovery
gave title to the government by whose subjects or by
whose authority it was made, against all other European
governments, which title might be consummated by possession."

This principle, acknowledged by all Europeans, because it
was the interest of all to acknowledge it, gave to the nation making the discovery, as its inevitable consequence,
the sole right of acquiring the soil and of making settlements on it. It was an exclusive principle which shut out
the right of competition among those who had agreed to
it; not one which could annul the previous rights of those
who had not agreed to it. It regulated the right given by
discovery among the European discoverers, but could not
affect the rights of those already in possession, either as
aboriginal occupants, or as occupants by virtue of a discovery made before the memory of man. It gave the exclusive right to purchase, but did not found that right on a
denial of the right of the possessor to sell.

The relation between the Europeans and the natives was
determined in each case by the particular government
which asserted and could maintain this pre-emptive privilege in the particular place. The United States succeeded
to all the claims of Great Britain, both territorial and political; but no attempt, so far as is known, has been made
to enlarge them. So far as they existed merely in theory,
or were in their nature only exclusive of the claims of
other European nations, they still retain their original
character, and remain dormant. So far as they have been
practically exerted, they exist in fact, are understood by

both parties, are asserted by the one, and admitted by the other.

Soon after Great Britain determined on planting colonies in America, the king granted charters to companies of his subjects, who associated for the purpose of carrying the views of the crown into effect, and of enriching themselves. The first of these charters was made before possession was taken of any part of the country. They purport, generally, to convey the soil, from the Atlantic to the South Sea. This soil was occupied by numerous and warlike nations, equally willing and able to defend their possessions. The extravagant and absurd idea that the feeble settlements made on the sea-coast, or the companies under whom they were made, acquired legitimate power by them to govern the people, or occupy the lands from sea to sea, did not enter the mind of any man. They were well understood to convey the title which, according to the common law of European sovereigns respecting America, they might rightfully convey, and no more. This was the exclusive right of purchasing such lands as the natives were willing to sell. The crown could not be understood to grant what the crown did not affect to claim, nor was it so understood.

The power of making war is conferred by these charters on the colonies, but defensive war alone seems to have been contemplated. In the first charter to the first and second colonies, they are empowered, "for their several defenses, to encounter, expulse, repel, and resist, all persons who shall, without license," attempt to inhabit "within the said precincts and limits of the said several colonies, or that shall enterprise or attempt at any time hereafter the least detriment or annoyance of the said several colonies or plantations."

. . . . These motives for planting the new colony are incompatible with the lofty ideas of granting the soil and all its inhabitants from sea to sea. They demonstrate the truth that these grants asserted a title against Europeans only, and were considered as blank paper so far as the rights of the natives were concerned. The power of war is given only for defense, not for conquest.

The charters contain passages showing one of their objects to be the civilization of the Indians and their conversion to Christianity - objects to be accomplished by conciliatory conduct and good example; not by extermination.

. . . . Certain it is, that our history furnishes no example, from the first settlement of our country, of any attempt on the part of the crown to interfere with the internal affairs of the Indians, farther than to keep out the agents of foreign powers, who, as traders or otherwise, might seduce them into foreign alliances. The king purchased their lands when they were willing to sell, at a price they were willing to take; but never coerced a surrender of them. He also purchased their alliance and dependence by subsidies; but never intruded into the interior of their affairs, or interfered with their self-government, so far as respected themselves only.

. . . . Such was the policy of Great Britain towards the Indian nations inhabiting the territory from which she excluded all other Europeans; such her claims, and such her practical exposition of the charters she had granted: she considered them as nations capable of maintaining the relations of peace and war; of governing themselves, under her protection; and she made treaties with them, the obligation of which she acknowledged.

This was the settled state of things when the war of our Revolution commenced. The influence of our enemy was established; her resources enabled her to keep up that influence, and the colonists had much cause for the apprehension that the Indian nations would, as the allies of Great Britain, add their arms to hers. This, as was to be expected, became an object of great solicitude to Congress. Far from advancing a claim to their lands, or asserting any right of dominion over them, Congress resolved "that the securing and preserving the friendship of the Indian nations appears to be a subject of the utmost moment to these colonies."

The early journals of Congress exhibit the most anxious desire to conciliate the Indian nations. Three Indian departments were established, and commissioners appointed in each, "to treat with the Indians in their respective departments, in the name and on the behalf of the United Colonies, in order to preserve peace and friendship with the said Indians, and to prevent their taking any part in the present commotions."

The most strenuous exertions were made to procure those supplies on which Indian friendships were supposed to depend; and everything which might excite hostility was avoided.

The first treaty was made with the Delawares, in September, 1778.

The language of equality in which it is drawn evinces the temper with which the negotiation was undertaken, and the opinion which then prevailed in the United States.

. . . . During the war of the Revolution, the Cherokees took part with the British. After its termination, the United States, though desirous of peace, did not feel its necessity so strongly as while the war continued. Their political situation being changed, they might very well think it advisable to assume a higher tone, and to impress on the Cherokees the same respect for Congress which was before felt for the King of Great Britain. This may account for the language of the Treaty of Hopewell. There is the more reason for supposing that the Cherokee chiefs were not very critical judges of the language, from the fact that every one makes his mark; no chief was capable of signing his name. It is probable the treaty was interpreted to them.

The treaty is introduced with the declaration that "the commissioners plenipotentiary of the United States give peace to all the Cherokees, and receive them into the favor and protection of the United States of America. . . ."

The general law of European sovereigns, respecting their claims in America, limited the intercourse of Indians, in a great degree, to the particular potentate whose ultimate right of domain was acknowledged by the others. This was the general state of things in time of peace. It was sometimes changed in war. The consequence was that their supplies were derived chiefly from that nation, and their trade confined to it. Goods, indispensable to their comfort, in the shape of presents, were received from the same hand. What was of still more importance, the strong hand of government was interposed to restrain the disorderly and licentious from intrusions into their country, from encroachments on their lands, and from those acts of violence which were often attended by reciprocal murder. The Indians perceived in this protection only what was beneficial to themselves - an engagement to punish aggressions on them. It involved, practically, no claim to their lands, no dominion over their persons. It merely bound the nation to the British crown as a dependent ally, claiming the protection of a powerful friend and neighbor, and receiving the advantages of that protection, without involving a surrender of their national character.

This is the true meaning of the stipulation, and is undoubtedly the sense in which it was made. Neither the British government nor the Cherokees ever understood it otherwise.

The same stipulation entered into with the United States, is undoubtedly to be [interpreted] in the same manner. They receive the Cherokee Nation into their favor and protection. The Cherokees acknowledge themselves to be under the protection of the United States, and of no other power. Protection does not imply the destruction of the protected. . . .

The treaty of Hopewell seems not to have established a solid peace. To accommodate the differences still existing between the State of Georgia and the Cherokee Nation, the Treaty of Holston was negotiated in July, 1791. The existing Constitution of the United States had been then adopted, and the government, having more intrinsic capacity to enforce its just claims, was perhaps less mindful of high sounding expressions denoting superiority. We hear no more of giving peace to the Cherokees. The mutual desire of establishing permanent peace and friendship, and of removing all causes of war, is honestly avowed, and, in pursuance of this desire, the first article declares that there shall be perpetual peace and friendship between all

the citizens of the United States of America and all the
individuals composing the Cherokee Nation.

The second article repeats the important acknowledgment
that the Cherokee Nation is under the protection of the
United States of America, and of no other sovereign
whosoever.

. . . . The Indian nations were, from their situation, necessarily dependent on some foreign potentate for the supply
of their essential wants, and for their protection from law-
less and injurious intrusions into their country. That power was naturally termed their protector. They had been
arranged under the protection of Great Britain; but the
extinguishment of the British power in their neighbor-
hood, and the establishment of that of the United States in
its place, led naturally to the declaration, on the part of
the Cherokees, that they were under the protection of the
United States, and of no other power. They assumed the
relation with the United States which had before subsisted
with Great Britain.

This relation was that of a nation claiming and receiving
the protection of one more powerful, not that of individuals abandoning their national character, and submitting as
subjects to the laws of a master.

. . . . From the commencement of our government Congress has passed acts to regulate trade and intercourse
with the Indians; which treat them as nations, respect
their rights, and manifest a firm purpose to afford that
protection which treaties stipulate. All these acts, and especially that of 1802, which is still in force, manifestly
consider the several Indian nations as distinct political
communities, having territorial boundaries, within which

their authority is exclusive, and having a right to all the lands within those boundaries, which is not only acknowledged, but guaranteed by the United States.

In 1819, Congress passed an Act for promoting those humane designs of civilizing the neighboring Indians, which had long been cherished by the executive. It enacts, "that, for the purpose of providing against the further decline and final extinction of the Indian tribes adjoining to the frontier settlements of the United States, and for introducing among them the habits and arts of civilization, the President of the United States shall be, and he is hereby authorized, in every case where he shall judge improvement in the habits and condition of such Indians practicable, and that the means of instruction can be introduced with their own consent, to employ capable persons, of good moral character, to instruct them in the mode of agriculture suited to their situation; and for teaching their children in reading, writing and arithmetic; and for performing such other duties as may be enjoined, according to such instructions and rules as the President may give and prescribe for the regulation of their conduct in the discharge of their duties."

This act avowedly contemplates the preservation of the Indian nations as an object sought by the United States, and proposes to effect this object by civilizing and converting them from hunters into agriculturists. Though the Cherokees had already made considerable progress in this improvement, it cannot be doubted that the general words of the act comprehend them. Their advance in the "habits and arts of civilization," rather encouraged perseverance in the laudable exertions still farther to meliorate their condition. This act furnishes strong additional evidence of a settled purpose to fix the Indians in their country by giving them security at home.

The treaties and laws of the United States contemplate the Indian territory as completely separated from that of the States; and provide that all intercourse with them shall be carried on exclusively by the government of the Union. Is this the rightful exercise of power, or is it usurpation?

While these States were colonies, this power, in its utmost extent, was admitted to reside in the crown. When our revolutionary struggle commenced, Congress was composed of an assemblage of deputies acting under specific powers granted by the legislatures, or conventions of the several colonies. It was a great popular movement, not perfectly organized; nor were the respective powers of those who were intrusted with the management of affairs accurately defined. The necessities of our situation produced a general conviction that those measures which concerned all, must be transacted by a body in which the representatives of all were assembled, and which could command the confidence of all: Congress, therefore, was considered as invested with all the powers of war and peace, and Congress dissolved our connection with the mother country, and declared these United Colonies to be independent States. Without any written definition of powers, they employed diplomatic agents to represent the United States at the several courts of Europe; offered to negotiate treaties with them, and did actually negotiate treaties with France. From the same necessity, and on the same principles, Congress assumed the management of Indian affairs; first in the name of these United Colonies, and afterwards in the name of the United States. Early attempts were made at negotiation, and to regulate trade with them. These not proving successful, war was carried on under the direction, and with the forces of the United States, and the efforts to make peace by treaty were earnest and incessant. The confederation found Congress in the exercise of the same powers of peace and war, in our relations with Indian nations, as with those of Europe.

Such was the state of things when the confederation was adopted. That instrument surrendered the powers of peace and war to Congress and prohibited them to the States, respectively, unless a State be actually invaded, "or shall have received certain advice of a resolution being formed by some nation of Indians to invade such State, and the danger is so imminent as not to admit of delay till the United States in Congress assembled can be consulted." This instrument also gave the United States in Congress assembled the sole and exclusive right of "regulating the trade and managing all the affairs with the Indians, not members of any of the States: provided that the legislative power of any State within its own limits be not infringed or violated."

The ambiguous phrases which follow the grant of power to the United States were so construed by the States of North Carolina and Georgia as to annul the power itself. The discontents and confusion resulting from these conflicting claims produced representations to Congress, which were referred to a committee, who made their report in 1787. The report does not assent to the construction of the two States, but recommends an accommodation, by liberal cessions of territory, or by an admission on their part of the powers claimed by Congress. The correct exposition of this article is rendered unnecessary by the adoption of our existing Constitution. That instrument confers on Congress the powers of war and peace; of making treaties, and of regulating commerce with foreign nations, and among the several States, and with the Indian tribes. These powers comprehend all that is required for the regulation of our intercourse with the Indians. They are not limited by any restrictions on their free actions. The shackles imposed on this power, in the confederation, are discarded.

The Indian nations had always been considered as distinct, independent political communities, retaining their original natural rights, as the undisputed possessors of the soil from time immemorial, with the single exception of that imposed by irresistible power, which excluded them from intercourse with any other European potentate than the first discoverer of the coast of the particular region claimed: and this was a restriction which those European potentates imposed on themselves, as well as on the Indians. The very term "nation," so generally applied to them, means "a people distinct from others." The Constitution, by declaring treaties already made, as well as those to be made, to be the supreme law of the land, has adopted and sanctioned the previous treaties with the Indian nations, and consequently admits their rank among those powers who are capable of making treaties. The words "treaty" and "nation" are words of our own language, selected in our diplomatic and legislative proceedings, by ourselves, having each a definite and well understood meaning. We have applied them to Indians, as we have applied them to the other nations of the earth. They are applied to all in the same sense.

Georgia herself has furnished conclusive evidence that her former opinions on this subject concurred with those entertained by her sister States, and by the government of the United States. Various acts of her Legislature have been cited in the argument, including the contract of ces-

sion made in the year 1802, all tending to prove her ac-
quiescence in the universal conviction that the Indian nations possessed a full right to the lands they occupied, until that right should be extinguished by the United States,
with their consent; that their territory was separated from
that of any State within whose chartered limits they might
reside, by a boundary line, established by treaties; that,
within their boundary, they possessed rights with which
no State could interfere, and that the whole power of regulating the intercourse with them was vested in the United States. . . . Her new series of laws, manifesting her
abandonment of these opinions, appears to have commenced in December, 1828.

In opposition to this original right, possessed by the undisputed occupants of every country; to this recognition of
that right, which is evidenced by our history, in every
change through which we have passed, is placed the charters granted by the monarch of a distant and distinct region, parceling out a territory in possession of others
whom he could not remove and did not attempt to remove, and the cession made of his claims by the Treaty of
Peace.

The actual state of things at the time, and all history since,
explain these charters; and the King of Great Britain, at
the Treaty of Peace, could cede only what belonged to his
crown. These newly asserted titles can derive no aid from
the articles so often repeated in Indian treaties; extending
to them, first, the protection of Great Britain, and afterwards that of the United States. These articles are associated with others, recognizing their title to self-
government. The very fact of repeated treaties with them
recognizes it; and the settled doctrine of the law of nations is that a weaker power does not surrender its inde-

pendence - its right to self-government, by associating with a stronger and taking its protection. A weak State in order to provide for its safety, may place itself under the protection of one more powerful without stripping itself of the right of government, and ceasing to be a State. Examples of this kind are not wanting in Europe. "Tributary and feudatory states," says Vattel, "do not thereby cease to be sovereign and independent states so long as self-government and sovereign and independent authority are left in the administration of the state." At the present day, more than one State may be considered as holding its right of self-government under the guaranty and protection of one or more allies.

The Cherokee Nation, then, is a distinct community, occupying its own territory, with boundaries accurately described, in which the laws of Georgia can have no force, and which, the citizens of Georgia have no right to enter but with the assent of the Cherokees themselves or in conformity with treaties and with the acts of Congress. The whole intercourse between the United States and this nation is, by our Constitution and laws, vested in the government of the United States.

The act of the State of Georgia under which [Worcester] was prosecuted is consequently [null and] void. . . . Can this court revise and reverse it?

If the objection to the system of legislation lately adopted by the Legislature of Georgia in relation to the Cherokee Nation was confined to its extraterritorial operation, the objection, though complete, so far as respected mere right, would give this court no power over the subject. But it goes much further. If the review which has been taken be correct, and we think it is, the acts of Georgia are repugnant to the Constitution, laws, and treaties of the United States.

They interfere forcibly with the relations established between the United States and the Cherokee Nation, the regulation of which, according to the settled principles of our Constitution, are committed exclusively to the government of the Union.

They are in direct hostility with treaties, repeated in a succession of years, which mark out the boundary that separates the Cherokee country from Georgia; guaranty to them all the land within their boundary; solemnly pledge the faith of the United States to restrain their citizens from trespassing on it; and recognize the pre-existing power of the nation to govern itself.

They are in equal hostility with the acts of Congress for regulating this intercourse, and giving effect to the treaties.

The forcible seizure and abduction of [Worcester], who was residing in the nation with its permission, and by authority of the President of the United States, is also a violation of the acts which authorize the chief magistrate to exercise this authority.

Will these powerful considerations avail [Worcester]? We think they will. He was seized and forcibly carried away while under guardianship of treaties guarantying the country in which he resided, and taking it under the protection of the United States. He was seized while performing under the sanction of the chief magistrate of the Union those duties which the humane policy adopted by Congress had recommended. He was apprehended, tried, and condemned, under color of a law which has been shown to be repugnant to the Constitution, laws, and treaties of the United States. Had a judgment, liable to the same objections, been rendered for property, none would question the jurisdiction of this court. It cannot be less clear when the judgment affects personal liberty, and inflicts disgraceful punishment, if punishment could disgrace when inflicted on innocence. [Worcester] is not less interested in the operation of this unconstitutional law than if it affected his property. He is not less entitled to the protection of the Constitution, laws, and treaties of his country.

. . . . It is the opinion of this court that the judgment of the Superior Court for the County of Gwinnett, in the State of Georgia, condemning Samuel A. Worcester to hard labor in the penitentiary of the State of Georgia for four years, was pronounced by that court under color of a law which is void, as being repugnant to the Constitution, treaties, and laws of the United States, and ought, therefore, to be reversed and annulled.

Upon hearing Marshall's decision, it is said President Jackson replied: "John Marshall has made his decision, now let him enforce it." In 1838, on the pretext of a fraudulent 1835 Indian Treaty, President Jackson ordered the U.S. Army to expel the entire Cherokee Nation from Georgia to Indian Territory in present day Oklahoma. Jackson said: "Your white brothers will . . . have no claim to the land and you can live upon it, you and all your children, as long as the grass grows or the water runs, in peace and plenty. It will be yours forever." The terrible journey to the Indian Territory in which thousands died of exposure, hunger and disease was called by the Cherokees "The Trail of Tears."

LINCOLN'S SUSPENSION OF HABEAS CORPUS

In the Matter of Milligan

The privilege of the writ of habeas corpus shall not be suspended, unless when in cases of rebellion or invasion the public safety may require it.

Article 1, Section 9, Clause 2
United States Constitution

A Writ of Habeas Corpus is an order from a judge to a person imprisoning another. It requires that person to produce the prisoner and submit to the judgment of a court on whether the prisoner has been wrongfully imprisoned and should be released. On September 24, 1862 Abraham Lincoln, under the authority of the Constitution, suspended the writ of habeas corpus until the end of the Civil War. Lincoln wrote: "Must I shoot a simple-minded soldier boy who deserts, while I must not touch a hair of a wily agitator who induces him to desert? I think in such a case to silence the agitator and save the boy is not only constitutional, but withal a great mercy."

Lambdin Milligan, a "Copperhead" - a Northerner in sympathy with the South - was what Lincoln called a "wily agitator" who needed to be "silenced." On October 5, 1864 Milligan, an Indiana civilian, was arrested by the U.S. Army for conspiracy. Tried for treason by a military court, he was sentenced to hang. Milligan petitioned the Indiana Federal Court to issue a writ of habeas corpus. The Indiana Court divided on granting the writ and appealed to the United States Supreme Court.

Oral arguments commenced on March 5, 1866. David Dudley Field and James A. Garfield represented Milligan. Attorney General James Speed and U.S. Army General Benjamin Butler represented the United States. On December 17, 1866 Justice David Davis announced the 9-0 decision of the Court. The edited text follows.

THE MILLIGAN COURT

Chief Justice Salmon P. Chase
Appointed by President Lincoln
Served 1864 - 1873

Associate Justice James M. Wayne
Appointed by President Jackson
Served 1835 - 1867

Associate Justice Samuel Nelson
Appointed by President Tyler
Served 1845 - 1872

Associate Justice Robert C. Grier
Appointed by President Polk
Served 1846 - 1870

Associate Justice Nathan A. Clifford
Appointed by President Buchanan
Served 1858 - 1881

Associate Justice Noah H. Swayne
Appointed by President Lincoln
Served 1862 - 1881

Associate Justice Samuel F. Miller
Appointed by President Lincoln
Served 1862 - 1890

Associate Justice David Davis
Appointed by President Lincoln
Served 1862 - 1877

Associate Justice Stephen J. Field
Appointed by President Lincoln
Served 1863 - 1897

The unedited text of *In the Matter of Milligan* can be found on page 2, volume 71 of *United States Reports.*

IN THE MATTER OF
LAMBDIN P. MILLIGAN
DECEMBER 17, 1866

JUSTICE DAVIS: On the 10th day of May, 1865, Lambdin P. Milligan presented a petition to the Circuit Court
of the United States for the District of Indiana, to be discharged from an alleged unlawful imprisonment. The
case made by the petition is this: Milligan is a citizen of
the United States; has lived for twenty years in Indiana;
and, at the time of the grievances complained of, was not,
and never had been, in the military service of the United
States. On the 5th day of October, 1864, while at home,
he was arrested by order of [General] Alvin P. Hovey,
commanding the military district of Indiana; and has ever
since been kept in close confinement.

On the 21st day of October, 1864, he was brought before
a Military Commission, convened at Indianapolis, by order
of [General] Hovey, tried on certain charges and specifica-
tions; found guilty, and sentenced to be hanged; and the
sentence ordered to be executed on Friday, the 19th day
of May, 1865.

On the 2nd day of January, 1865, after the proceedings of
the Military Commission were at an end, the Circuit Court
of the United States for Indiana met at Indianapolis and
impaneled a grand jury, who were charged to inquire
whether the laws of the United States had been violated.
... The court adjourned on the 27th day of January, having, prior thereto, discharged from further service the
grand jury, who did not find any bill of indictment
[charge] or make any presentment against Milligan for
any offense whatever; and, in fact, since his imprison-

ment, no bill of indictment has been found or presentment made against him by any grand jury of the United
States.

Milligan insists that said Military Commission had no jurisdiction [authority] to try him upon the charges preferred, or upon any charge whatever; because he was a
citizen of the United States and the State of Indiana, and
had not been, since the commencement of the late Rebellion, a resident of any of the States whose citizens were
arrayed against the government, and that the right of trial
by jury was guaranteed to him by the constitution of the
United States.

The [petition asked] that under the Act of Congress, approved March 3rd, 1863, "An Act Relating to *Habeas Corpus* [an order to to bring a person before the court], and
Regulating Judicial Proceedings in certain Cases," he may
be brought before the court, and either turned over to the
proper civil tribunal to be proceeded against according to
the law of the land or discharged from custody altogether.

. . . The opinions of the judges of the circuit court were
opposed on three questions, which are certified [vouched
for], to the Supreme Court:

1st.   "On the facts stated in said petition and exhibits,
ought a writ of *habeas corpus* to be issued?"

2d.   "On the facts stated in said petition and exhibits,
ought the said Lambdin P. Milligan to be discharged from
custody?"

3d. "Whether, upon the facts stated in said petition and exhibits, the Military Commission mentioned therein had jurisdiction legally to try and sentence said Milligan." . . .

The importance of the main question presented by this record cannot be overstated: for it involves the very framework of the government and the fundamental principles of American liberty.

During the late wicked Rebellion, the temper of the times did not allow that calmness in deliberation and discussion so necessary to a correct conclusion of a purely judicial question. Then, considerations of safety were mingled with the exercise of power; and feelings and interests prevailed which are happily terminated. Now that the public safety is assured, this question, as well as all others, can be discussed and decided without passion or the admixture of any element not required to form a legal judgment. We approach the investigation of this case, fully sensible of the magnitude of the inquiry and the necessity of full and cautious deliberation.

. . . It was admitted . . . that the circuit court had jurisdiction to entertain the application for the writ of *habeas corpus*, and to hear and determine it; and it could not be denied; for the power is expressly given in the 14th section of the Judiciary Act of 1789, as well as in the latter Act of 1863. . . .

Milligan claimed his discharge from custody by virtue of the Act of Congress "Relating to *Habeas Corpus*, and Regulating Judicial Proceedings in Certain Cases," approved March 3d, 1863. Did that Act confer jurisdiction on the Circuit Court of Indiana to hear this case?

In interpreting a law, the motives which must have operated with the legislature in passing it are proper to be considered. This law was passed in a time of great national peril, when our heritage of free government was in danger. An armed rebellion against the national authority, of greater proportions than history affords an example of, was raging; and the public safety required that the privilege of the writ of *habeas corpus* should be suspended. The President had practically suspended it, and detained suspected persons in custody without trial; but his authority to do this was questioned. It was claimed that Congress alone could exercise this power; and that the Legislature, and not the President, should judge of the political considerations upon which the right to suspend it rested. The privilege of this great writ had never before been withheld from the citizen; and as the exigency of the times demanded immediate action, it was of the highest importance that the lawfulness of the suspension should be fully established. It was under these circumstances; which were such as to arrest the attention of the country, that this law was passed. The President was authorized by it to suspend the privilege of the writ of *habeas corpus*, whenever, in his judgment, the public safety required; and he did, by proclamation, bearing date the 15th of September, 1863, reciting, among other things, the authority of this statute, suspend it. The suspension of the writ does not authorize the arrest of any one, but simply denies to one arrested the privilege of this writ in order to obtain his liberty.

. . . . [I]t is said that this case is ended, as the presumption is that Milligan was hanged, in pursuance of the order of the President.

Although we have no judicial information on the subject, yet the inference is that he is alive; for otherwise learned counsel would not appear for him and urge this court to decide his case. It can never be in this country of written constitution and laws, with a Judicial Department to interpret them, that any chief magistrate would be so far forgetful of his duty, as to order the execution of a man who denied the jurisdiction that tried and convicted him; after his case was before federal judges with power to decide it, who, being unable to agree on the grave questions involved, had, according to known law, sent it to the Supreme Court of the United States for decision. But even the suggestion is injurious to the Executive, and we dismiss it from further consideration. There is, therefore, nothing to hinder this court from an investigation . . . of this controversy.

The controlling question in the case is this: Upon the facts stated in Milligan's petition, and the exhibits filed, had the Military Commission mentioned in it jurisdiction, legally, to try and sentence him? Milligan, not a resident of one of the rebellious States, or a prisoner of war, but a citizen of Indiana for twenty years past, and never in the military or naval service, is, while at his home, arrested by the military power of the United States, imprisoned and, on certain criminal charges preferred against him, tried, convicted and sentenced to be hanged by a military commission, organized under the direction of the military commander of the military district of Indiana. Had this tribunal the legal power and authority to try and punish this man?

No graver question was ever considered by this court, nor one which more nearly concerns the rights of the whole people; for it is the birthright of every American citizen when charged with crime, to be tried and punished according to law. The power of punishment is alone through the means which the laws have provided for that purpose, and if they are ineffectual, there is an immunity from punishment, no matter how great an offender the individual may be, or how much his crimes may have shocked the sense of justice of the country, or endangered its safety. By the protection of the law human rights are secured; withdraw that protection, and they are at the mercy of wicked rulers, or the clamor of an excited people. If there was law to justify this military trial, it is not our province to interfere; if there was not, it is our duty to declare the nullity of the whole proceedings. ... The founders of our government were familiar with the history of that struggle; and secured in a written Constitution every right which the people had wrested from power during a contest of ages. By that Constitution and the laws authorized by it, this question must be determined. The provisions of that instrument on the administration of criminal justice are too plain and direct to leave room for misconstruction or doubt of their true meaning. Those applicable to this case are found in that clause of the original Constitution which says, "That the trial of all crimes, except in case of impeachment, shall be by jury:" and in the fourth, fifth and sixth articles of the amendments. The fourth proclaims the right to be secure in person and effects against unreasonable search and seizure; and directs that a judicial warrant shall not issue "without proof of probable cause supported by oath or affirmation." The fifth declares "that no person shall be held to answer for a capital or otherwise infamous crime unless on presentment by a grand jury, except in cases arising in the land or naval forces, or in the militia, when in actual service in time of war or public danger, nor be deprived of life, liberty, or property, without due process

of law." And the sixth guarantees the right of trial by
jury, in such manner and with such regulations that with
upright judges, impartial juries, and an able bar, the innocent will be saved and the guilty punished. It is in these
words: "In all criminal prosecutions the accused shall enjoy the right to a speedy and public trial by an impartial
jury of the State and district wherein the crime shall have
been committed, which district shall have been previously
ascertained by law, and to be informed of the nature and
cause of the accusation; to be confronted with the witnesses against him; to have compulsory process for obtaining witnesses in his favor, and to have the assistance of
counsel for his defense." These securities for personal liberty thus embodied, were such as wisdom and experience
had demonstrated to be necessary for the protection of
those accused of crime. And so strong was the sense of
the country of their importance, and so jealous were the
people, that these rights, highly prized, might be denied
them by implication that when the original Constitution
was proposed for adoption it encountered severe opposition; and, but for the belief that it would be so amended
as to embrace them, it would never have been ratified.

Time has proven the discernment of our ancestors; for
even these provisions, expressed in such plain English
words, that it would seem the ingenuity of man could not
evade them, are now, after the lapse of more than seventy
years, sought to be avoided. Those great and good men
foresaw that troublous times would arise, when rulers and
people would become restive under restraint, and seek by
sharp and decisive measures to accomplish ends deemed
just and proper; and that the principles of constitutional
liberty would be in peril, unless established by irrepeal-
able law. The history of the world had taught them that
what was done in the past might be attempted in the fu-

ture. The Constitution of the United States is a law for
rulers and people, equally in war and in peace, and covers
with the shield of its protection all classes of men, at all
times, and under all circumstances. No doctrine, involving
more pernicious consequences, was ever invented by the
wit of man than that any of its provisions can be suspended during any of the great exigencies of government.
Such a doctrine leads directly to anarchy or despotism, but
the theory of necessity on which it is based is false; for
the government, within the Constitution, has all the powers granted to it which are necessary to preserve its existence, as has been happily proved by the result of the great
effort to throw off its just authority.

Have any of the rights guarantied by the Constitution
been violated in the case of Milligan? and if so, what are
they?

Every trial involves the exercise of judicial power; and
from what source did the Military Commission that tried
him derive their authority? Certainly no part of the judicial power of the country was conferred on them; because
the Constitution expressly vests it "in one Supreme Court
and such inferior courts as the Congress may from time to
time ordain and establish," and it is not pretended that the
commission was a court ordained and established by Congress. They cannot justify on the mandate of the President; because he is controlled by law, and has his appropriate sphere of duty, which is to execute, not to make,
the laws; and there is "no unwritten criminal code to
which resort can be had as a source of jurisdiction." But
it is said that the jurisdiction is complete under the "laws
and usages of war."

It can serve no useful purpose to inquire what those laws and usages are, whence they originated, where found, and on whom they operate; they can never be applied to citizens in States which have upheld the authority of the government, and where the courts are open and their process unobstructed. This court has judicial knowledge that in Indiana the federal authority was always unopposed, and its courts always open to hear criminal accusations and redress grievances; and no usage of war could sanction a military trial there for any offense whatever of a citizen in civil life, in nowise connected with the military service. Congress could grant no such power; and to the honor of our National Legislature be it said, it has never been provoked by the state of the country even to attempt its exercise. One of the plainest constitutional provisions was, therefore, infringed when Milligan was tried by a court not ordained and established by Congress, and not composed of judges appointed during good behavior.

Why was he not delivered to the Circuit Court of Indiana to be proceeded against according to law? No reason of necessity could be urged against it; because Congress had declared penalties against the offenses charged, provided for their punishment, and directed that court to hear and determine them. And soon after this military tribunal was ended, the circuit court met, peacefully transacted its business, and adjourned. It needed no bayonets to protect it, and required no military aid to execute its judgments. It was held in a State, eminently distinguished for patriotism, by judges commissioned during the Rebellion, who were provided with juries, upright, intelligent, and selected by a Marshal appointed by the President. The government had no right to conclude that Milligan, if guilty, would not receive in that court merited punishment; for its records disclose that it was constantly engaged in the trial of similar offenses, and was never interrupted in its administration of criminal justice. If it was dangerous, in the distracted condition of affairs, to leave Milligan unrestrained of his liberty, because he "conspired against the government, afforded aid and comfort to rebels, and incited the people to insurrection," the law said arrest him, confine him closely, render him powerless to do further mischief; and then present his case to the grand jury of the district, with proofs of his guilt and, if indicted, try him according to the course of the common law. If this had been done, the Constitution would have been vindicated, the Law of 1863 enforced, and the securities for personal liberty preserved and defended.

Another guarantee of freedom was broken when Milligan was denied a trial by jury. The great minds of the country have differed on the correct interpretation to be given to various provisions of the Federal Constitution; and judicial decision has been often invoked to settle their true meaning; but until recently no one ever doubted that the right of trial by jury was fortified in the organic law against the power of attack. It is now assailed; but if ideas can be expressed in words, and language has any meaning, this right - one of the most valuable in a free country - is preserved to every one accused of crime who is not attached to the army or navy or militia in actual service. The sixth amendment affirms that "in all criminal prosecutions the accused shall enjoy the right to a speedy and public trial by an impartial jury," language broad enough to embrace all persons and cases; but the fifth, recognizing the necessity of an indictment, or presentment, before anyone can be held to answer for high crimes, "excepts cases arising in the land or naval forces, or in the militia, when in actual service, in time of war or public danger;" and the framers of the Constitution, doubtless, meant to limit the right of trial by jury, in the sixth amendment, to those persons who were subject to indictment or presentment in the fifth.

The discipline necessary to the efficiency of the army and navy, required other and swifter modes of trial than are furnished by the common law courts; and, in pursuance of the power conferred by the Constitution, Congress has declared the kinds of trial and the manner in which they shall be conducted, for offenses committed while the party is in the military or naval service. Every one connected with these branches of public service is amenable to the jurisdiction which Congress has created for their government, and, while thus serving, surrenders his right to be tried by the civil courts. All other persons, citizens of States where the courts are open, if charged with crime, are guarantied the inestimable privilege of trial by jury. This privilege is a vital principle, underlying the whole administration of criminal justice; it is not held by sufferance, and cannot be frittered away on any plea of state or political necessity. When peace prevails, and the authority of the government is undisputed, there is no difficulty in preserving the safeguards of liberty; for the ordinary modes of trial are never neglected, and no one wishes it otherwise; but if society is disturbed by civil commotion - if the passions of men are aroused and the restraints of law weakened, if not disregarded - these safeguards need, and should receive, the watchful care of those intrusted with the guardianship of the Constitution and laws. In no other way can we transmit to posterity unimpaired the blessings of liberty, consecrated by the sacrifices of the Revolution.

. . . . This nation, as experience has proved, cannot always remain at peace, and has no right to expect that it will always have wise and humane rulers, sincerely attached to the principles of the Constitution. Wicked men, ambitious of power, with hatred of liberty and contempt of law, may fill the place once occupied by Washington and Lincoln; and if this right is conceded, and the calamities of war again befall us, the dangers to human liberty are frightful to contemplate. If our fathers had failed to provide for just such a contingency, they would have been false to the trust reposed in them. They knew - the history of the world told them - the nation they were founding, be its existence short or long, would be involved in war; how often or how long continued, human foresight could not tell; and that unlimited power, wherever lodged at such a time, was especially hazardous to freemen. For this, and other equally weighty reasons, they secured the inheritance they had fought to maintain, by incorporating in a written Constitution the safeguards which time had proved were essential to its preservation. Not one of these safeguards can the President or Congress or the Judiciary disturb, except the one concerning the writ of *habeas corpus.*

It is essential to the safety of every government that, in a great crisis, like the one we have just passed through, there should be a power somewhere of suspending the writ of *habeas corpus.* In every war, there are men of previously good character, wicked enough to counsel their fellow citizens to resist the measures deemed necessary by a good government to sustain its just authority and overthrow its enemies; and their influence may lead to dangerous combinations. In the emergency of the times, as immediate public investigation according to law my not be possible; and yet, the peril to the country may be too imminent to suffer such persons to go at large. Unquestionably, there is then an exigency which demands that the government, if it should see fit, in the exercise of a proper discretion, to make arrests, should not be required to produce the person arrested in answer to a writ of *habeas corpus*. The Constitution goes no further. It does not say after a writ of *habeas corpus* is denied a citizen, that he shall be tried otherwise than by the course of common law. If it had intended this result, it was easy by the use of direct words to have accomplished it. The illustrious men who framed that instrument were guarding the foundations of civil liberty against the abuses of unlimited power; they were full of wisdom, and the lessons of history informed them that a trial by an established court, assisted by an impartial jury, was the only sure way of protecting the citizen against oppression and wrong. Knowing this, they limited the suspension to one great right, and left the rest to remain forever inviolable. But it is insisted that the safety of the country in time of war demands that this broad claim for martial law shall be sustained. If this were true, it could be well said that a country, preserved at the sacrifice of all the cardinal principles of liberty, is not worth the cost of preservation. Happily, it is not so.

. . . . So sensitive were our Revolutionary fathers on this subject, although Boston was almost in a state of siege, when General Gage issued his proclamation of martial law, they spoke of it as an "attempt to supersede the course of the common law, and instead thereof to publish and order the use of martial law." The Virginia Assembly, also, denounced a similar measure on the part of Governor Dunmore "as an assumed power, which the King himself cannot exercise; because it annuls the law of the land and introduces the most execrable of all systems, martial law."

In some parts of the country, during the war of 1812, our officers made arbitrary arrests and, by military tribunals, tried citizens who were not in the military service. These arrests, and trials, when brought to the notice of the courts, were uniformly condemned as illegal. . . .

To the third question, then, on which the judges [of the courts] below were opposed in opinion, an answer in the negative must be returned.

It is proper to say, although Milligan's trial and conviction by a military commission was illegal, yet, if guilty of the crimes imputed to him, and his guilt had been ascertained by an established court and impartial jury, he deserved severe punishment. Open resistance to the measures deemed necessary to subdue a great rebellion by those who enjoy the protection of government . . . is wicked, but that resistance becomes an enormous crime when it assumes the form of a secret political organization, armed to oppose the laws, and seeks by stealthy means to introduce the enemies of the country into peaceful communities, there to light the torch of civil war, and thus overthrow the power of the United States. Conspiracies like these, at such a juncture, are extremely perilous; and those concerned in them are dangerous enemies to their country and should receive the heaviest penalties of the law, as an example to deter others from similar criminal conduct. It is said the severity of the laws caused them; but Congress was obliged to enact severe laws to meet the crisis; and as our highest civil duty is to serve our country when in danger, the late war has proved that rigorous laws, when necessary, will be cheerfully obeyed by a patriotic people, struggling to preserve the rich blessings of a free government.

The two remaining questions in this case must be answered in the affirmative. The suspension of the privilege of the writ of *habeas corpus* does not suspend the writ itself. The writ issues as a matter of course; and on the return made to it the court decides whether the party applying is denied the right of proceeding any further with it.

If the military trail of Milligan was contrary to law, then he was entitled, on the facts stated in his petition, to be discharged from custody by the terms of the Act of Congress of March 3d, 1863. Milligan avers he was a citizen of Indiana, not in the military or naval service, and was detained in close confinement, by order of the President, from the 5th day of October, 1864, until the 2d day of January, 1865, when the Circuit Court for the District of Indiana, with a grand jury, convened in session at Indianapolis; and afterwards, on the 27th day of the same month, adjourned without finding an indictment or presentment against him. If these averments were true (and their truth is conceded for the purposes of this case), the court was required to liberate him on taking certain oaths prescribed by the law, and entering into recognizance for his good behavior.

But it is insisted that Milligan was a prisoner of war and, therefore, excluded from the privileges of the statute. It is not easy to see how he can be treated as a prisoner of war, when he lived in Indiana for the past twenty years, was arrested there, and had not been, during the late troubles, a resident of any of the States in rebellion. If in Indiana he conspired with bad men to assist the enemy, he is punishable for it in the courts of Indiana; but, when tried for the offense, he cannot plead the rights of war; for he was not engaged in legal acts of hostility against the gov-

ernment, and only such persons, when captured, are pris-
oners of war. If he cannot enjoy the immunities attaching
to the character of a prisoner of war, how can he be subject to their pains and penalties? . . .

*Freed from military captivity by the United States Su-
preme Court, Lambdin P. Milligan sued the United States
Army for false imprisonment. An unsympathetic jury
awarded Milligan damages in the amount of $5.*

SEPARATE BUT EQUAL

Plessy v. Ferguson

All railway companies carrying passengers in their coaches in this state shall provide equal but separate accommodations for the white and colored races.

An Act of Louisiana, July 10, 1890

In the post-Civil War South, "Jim Crow" segregation laws were enacted by several states to counter the integration effects of the Thirteenth and Fourteenth Amendments to the United States Constitution.

In 1890 Louisiana enacted a "Jim Crow" law providing separate railway carriages for white and colored races. On June 7, 1892 Homer Adolph Plessy, a Louisianan of mixed descent (seven-eighths Caucasian and one-eighth African) purchased a first-class ticket in New Orleans on the East Louisiana Railway. Plessy, whose African descent was said not to be discernible in him, took a seat in a whites-only passenger coach. The conductor, told of Plessy's African descent, ordered Plessy to a colored-only coach. Plessy refused. The police were called. Plessy was ejected from the train and imprisoned for violation of Louisiana's "Jim Crow" law of July 10, 1890. Plessy, brought before John H. Ferguson, Judge of the Criminal Court for the Parish of Orleans, refused either to plead or to identify his race, asserting the July 10th law was an unconstitutional act. Plessy filed a petition to prohibit further proceedings by Judge Ferguson. The Louisiana Supreme Court held for the Judge. Plessy then appealed to the United States Supreme Court.

Oral arguments were heard April 13, 1896. On May 18, 1896 Justice Henry Billings Brown announced the 8-1 decision of the Court. Edited texts of Justice Brown's majority decision and Justice John Marshall Harlan's dissent follow.

THE PLESSY COURT

Chief Justice Melville W. Fuller
Appointed by President Cleveland
Served 1888 - 1901

Associate Justice Stephen J. Field
Appointed by President Lincoln
Served 1863 - 1897

Associate Justice John Marshall Harlan
Appointed by President Hays
Served 1877 - 1911

Associate Justice Horace Grey
Appointed by President Arthur
Served 1881- 1902

Associate Justice Henry B. Brown
Appointed by President Harrison
Served 1890 - 1906

Associate Justice George Shiras, Jr.
Appointed by President Harrison
Served 1892 - 1903

Associate Justice Edward D. White
Appointed Associate Justice by President Cleveland
Appointed Chief Justice by President Taft
Served 1894 - 1921

Associate Justice Rufus W. Peckham
Appointed by President Cleveland
Served 1895 - 1909

The unedited text of *Plessy v. Ferguson* can be found
on page 537, volume 163 of *United States Reports.*

PLESSY v. FERGUSON
MAY 18, 1896

JUSTICE BROWN: This case turns upon the constitutionality of an act of the general assembly of the state of Louisiana, passed in 1890, providing for separate railway carriages for the white and colored races.

The 1st section of the statute enacts "that all railway companies carrying passengers in their coaches in this state shall provide equal but separate accommodations for the white and colored races, by providing two or more passenger coaches for each passenger train, or by dividing the passenger coaches by a partition so as to secure separate accommodations: *Provided,* That this section shall not be construed [interpreted] to apply to street railroads. No person or persons shall be permitted to occupy seats in coaches other than the ones assigned to them, on account of the race they belong to."

By the 2d section it was enacted "that the officers of such passenger trains shall have power and are hereby required to assign each passenger to the coach or compartment used for the race to which such passenger belongs; any passenger insisting on going into a coach or compartment to which by race he does not belong, shall be liable to a fine of $25 or in lieu thereof to imprisonment for a period of not more than twenty days in the parish prison, and any officer of any railroad insisting on assigning a passenger to a coach or compartment other than the one set aside for the race to which said passenger belongs, shall be liable to a fine of $25, or in lieu thereof to imprisonment for a period of not more than twenty days in the parish prison; and should any passenger refuse to occupy the coach or compartment to which he or she is assigned by

the officer of such railway, said officer shall have power
to refuse to carry such passenger on his train, and for
such refusal neither he nor the railway company which he
represents shall be liable for damages in any of the courts
of this state."

The 3d section provides penalties for the refusal or neglect of the officers, directors, conductors, and employees
of railway companies to comply with the act, with a
proviso that "nothing in this act shall be construed as applying to nurses attending children of the other race." . . .

The information filed in the criminal district court
charged in substance that Plessy, being a passenger between two stations within the state of Louisiana, was assigned by officers of the company to the coach used for
the race to which he belonged, but he insisted upon going
into a coach used by the race to which he did not belong.
[Nowhere] was his particular race or color [indicated].

The petition [request to the court] . . . averred [declared]
that petitioner [Plessy] was seven eighths Caucasian and
one eighth African blood; that the mixture of colored
blood was not discernible in him, and that he was entitled
to every right, privilege, and immunity secured to citizens
of the United States of the white race; and that, upon such
theory, he took a possession of a vacant seat in a coach
where passengers of the white race were accommodated,
and was ordered by the conductor to vacate said coach and
take a seat in another assigned to persons of the colored
race, and having refused to comply with such demand he
was forcibly ejected with the aid of a police officer, and
imprisoned in the parish jail to answer a charge of having
violated the above act.

The constitutionality of this act is attacked upon the ground that it conflicts both with the 13th Amendment of the Constitution, abolishing slavery, and the 14th Amendment, which prohibits certain restrictive legislation on the part of the states.

That it does not conflict with the 13th Amendment,which abolished slavery and involuntary servitude, except as a punishment for crime, is too clear for argument. Slavery implies involuntary servitude - a state of bondage; the ownership of mankind as a chattel, or at least the control of the labor and services of one man for the benefit of another, and the absence of a legal right to the disposal of his own person, property, and services. This amendment was said in *Butcher's Benevolent Association v. Crescent City Slaughter House Co. ("Slaughterhouse Cases")*, to have been intended primarily to abolish slavery, as it had been previously known in this country, and that it equally forbade Mexican peonage or the Chinese coolie trade when they amounted to slavery or involuntary servitude, and that the use of the word "servitude" was intended to prohibit the use of all forms of involuntary slavery, of whatever class or name. It was intimated, however, in that case, that this amendment was regarded by the statesmen of that day as insufficient to protect the colored race from certain laws which had been enacted in the southern states, imposing upon the colored race onerous disabilities and burdens, and curtailing their rights in the pursuit of life, liberty, and property to such an extent that their freedom was of little value; and that the 14th Amendment was devised to meet this exigency.

So, too, in *United States v. Stanley ("Civil Rights Cases")*, it was said that the act of a mere individual, the owner of an inn, a public conveyance, or place of amusement, refus-

ing accommodations to colored people, cannot be justly regarded as imposing any badge of slavery or servitude
upon the applicant, but only as involving an ordinary civil
injury, properly cognizable by the laws of the state, and
presumably subject to redress by those laws until the contrary appears. "It would be running the slavery argument
into the ground," said Justice Bradley, "to make it apply to
every act of discrimination which a person may see fit to
make as to the guests he will entertain, or as to the people
he will take into his coach or cab or car, or admit to his
concert or theater, or deal with in other matters of intercourse or business."

A statute which implies merely a legal distinction between
the white and colored races - a distinction which is founded in the color of the two races, and which must always
exist so long as white men are distinguished from the other race by color - has no tendency to destroy the legal
equality of the two races, or reestablish a state of involuntary servitude. Indeed, we do not understand that the
13th Amendment is strenuously relied upon by [Plessy] in
this connection.

By the 14th Amendment, all persons born or naturalized
in the United States, and subject to the jurisdiction thereof, are made citizens of the United States, and of the state
wherein they reside; and the states are forbidden from
making or enforcing any law which shall abridge the
privileges or immunities of citizens of the United States,
or shall deprive any person of life, liberty, or property
without due process of law, or deny to any person within
their jurisdiction the equal protection of the laws.

The proper construction of this amendment was first
called to the attention of this court in the *Slaughterhouse*

Cases, which involved, however, not a question of race, but one of exclusive privileges. The case did not call for any expression of opinion as to the exact rights it was intended to secure to the colored race, but it was said generally that its main purpose was to establish the citizenship of the negro; to give definitions of citizenship of the United States and of the states, and to protect from the hostile legislation of the states the privileges and immunities of citizens of the United States, as distinguished from those of citizens of the states.

The object of the amendment was undoubtedly to enforce the absolute equality of the two races before the law, but in the nature of things it could not have been intended to abolish distinctions based upon color, or to enforce social, as distinguished from political, equality, or a commingling of the two races upon terms unsatisfactory to either. Laws permitting, and even requiring their separation in places where they are liable to be brought into contact do not necessarily imply the inferiority of either race to the other, and have been generally, if not universally, recognized as within the competency of the state legislatures in the exercise of their police power. The most common instance of this is connected with the establishment of separate schools for white and colored children, which have been held to be a valid exercise of the legislative power even by courts of states where the political rights of the colored race have been longest and most earnestly enforced.

One of the earliest of these cases is that of *Roberts v. Boston,* in which the supreme judicial court of Massachusetts held that the general school committee of Boston had power to make provision for the instruction of colored children in separate schools established exclusively for them, and to prohibit their attendance upon the other schools. "The great principle," said Chief Justice Shaw, "advanced by the learned and eloquent advocate of the plaintiff [Mr. Charles Sumner] is, that by the Constitution and laws of Massachusetts, all persons without distinction of age or sex, birth or color, origin or condition, are equal before the law. . . . But, when this great principle comes to be applied to the actual and various conditions of persons in society, it will not warrant the assertion that men and women are legally clothed with the same civil and political powers, and that children and adults are legally to have the same functions and be subject to the same treatment; but only that the rights of all, as they are settled and regulated by law, are equally entitled to the paternal consideration and protection of the law for their maintenance and security." It was held that the powers of the committee extended to the "establishment of separate schools for children of different ages, sexes, and colors, and that they might also establish special schools for poor and neglected children, who have become too old to attend the primary school, and yet have not acquired the rudiments of learning, to enable them to enter the ordinary schools. Similar laws have been enacted by Congress under its general power of legislation over the District of Columbia, as well as by the legislatures of many of the states, and have been generally, if not uniformly, sustained [maintained] by the courts.

Laws forbidding the intermarriage of the two races may be said in a technical sense to interfere with the freedom of contract, and yet have been universally recognized as within the police power of the state.

The distinction between laws interfering with the political equality of the negro and those requiring the separation of the two races in schools, theaters, and railway carriages, has been frequently drawn by this court. Thus, in *Strauder v. West Virginia*, it was held that a law of West Virginia limiting to white male persons, twenty-one years of age and citizens of the state, the right to sit upon juries, was a discrimination which implied a legal inferiority in civil society, which lessened the security of the right of the colored race, and was a step towards reducing them to a condition of servility. Indeed, the right of a colored man that, in the selection of jurors to pass upon his life, liberty, and property, there shall be no exclusion of his race and no discrimination against them because of color, has been asserted in a number of cases. So, where the laws of a particular locality or the charter of a particular railway corporation has provided that no person shall be excluded from the cars on account of color, we have held that this meant that persons of color should travel in the same car as white ones, and that the enactment was not satisfied by the company providing cars assigned exclusively to people of color, though they were as good as those which they assigned exclusively to white persons.

Upon the other hand, where a statute of Louisiana required those engaged in the transportation of passengers among the states to give to all persons traveling within that state, upon vessels employed in that business, equal rights and privileges in all parts of the vessel, without distinction on account of race or color, and subjected to an action for damages, the owner of such a vessel, who excluded colored passengers on account of their color from the cabin set aside by him for the use of whites, it was held to be, so far as it applied to interstate commerce, unconstitutional and void. The court in this case, however, expressly disclaimed that it had anything whatever to do with the statute as a regulation of internal commerce, or affecting anything else than commerce among the states.

In *United States v. Stanley*, it was held that an act of Congress, entitling all persons within the jurisdiction of the United States to the full and equal enjoyment of the accommodations, advantages, facilities, and privileges of inns, public conveyances on land or water, theaters, and other places of public amusement, and made applicable to citizens of every race and color, regardless of any previous condition of servitude, was unconstitutional and void upon the ground that the 14th Amendment was prohibitory upon the states only, and the legislation authorized to be adopted by Congress for enforcing it was not direct legislation on matters respecting which the states were prohibited from making or enforcing certain laws or doing certain acts, but was corrective legislation such as might be necessary or proper for counteracting and redressing the effect of such laws or acts. In delivering the opinion of the court Justice Bradley observed that the 14th Amendment "does not invest Congress with power to legislate upon subjects that are within the domain of state legislation; but to provide modes of relief against state legislation or state action, of the kind referred to. It does not authorize Congress to create a code of municipal law for the regulation of private rights; but to provide modes of redress against the operation of state laws, and the action of state officers, executive or judicial, when these are subversive of the fundamental rights specified in the amendment. Positive rights and privileges are undoubtedly secured by the 14th Amendment; but they are secured by way of prohibition against state laws and state proceedings affecting those rights and privileges, and by power given to Congress to legislate for the purpose of carrying such prohibition into effect; and such legislation must necessarily be predicated upon such supposed state laws or state proceedings, and be directed to the correction of their operation and effect."

Much nearer . . . is the case of the *Louisville Railroad Co. v. Mississippi*, wherein the railway company was indicted [charged] for a violation of a statute of Mississippi, enacting that all railroads carrying passengers should provide equal, but separate, accommodations for the white and colored races, by providing two or more passenger cars for each passenger train, or by dividing the passenger cars by a partition, so as to secure separate accommodations. The case was presented in a different aspect from the one under consideration, inasmuch as it was an indictment . . . against the railway company for failing to provide the separate accommodations, but the question considered was the constitutionality of the law. In that case, the supreme court of Mississippi, had held that the statute applied solely to commerce within the state, and, that being the construction of the state statue by its highest court, was accepted as conclusive. "If it be a matter," said the court, "respecting commerce wholly within a state, and not interfering with commerce between the states, then, obviously, there is no violation of the commerce clause of the Federal Constitution. . . . No question arises under this section as to the power of the state to separate in different compartments interstate passengers, or to affect, in any manner, the privileges and rights of such passengers. All that we can consider is, whether the state has the power to require that railroad trains within her limits shall have separate accommodations for the two races; that affecting only commerce within the state is no invasion of the powers given to Congress by the commerce clause."

A like course of reasoning applies to the case under consideration, since the supreme court of Louisiana in the case of *State, Abbot, v. Hicks,* held that the statute in question did not apply to interstate passengers, but was confined in its application to passengers traveling exclusively within the borders of the state. The case was decided largely upon the authority of *Louisville Railroad Co. v. State,* and affirmed [upheld] by this court. In the present case no question of interference with interstate commerce can possibly arise, since the East Louisiana Railway appears to have been purely a local line, with both its termini within the state of Louisiana. Similar statutes for the separation of the two races upon public conveyances [have been] held to be constitutional. . . .

While we think the enforced separation of the races, as applied to the internal commerce of the state, neither abridges the privileges or immunities of the colored man, deprives him of his property without due process of law, nor denies him the equal protection of the laws, within the meaning of the 14th Amendment, we are not prepared to say that the conductor, in assigning passengers to the coaches according to their race, does not act at this peril, or that the provision of the 2d section of the act that denies to the passenger compensation in damages for a refusal to receive him into the coach in which he properly belongs, is a valid exercise of the legislative power. Indeed, we understand it to be conceded by the state's attorney that such part of the act that exempts from liability the railway company and its officers is unconstitutional. The power to assign to a particular coach obviously implies the power to determine to which race the passenger belongs, as well as the power to determine who, under the laws of the particular state, is to be deemed a white and who a colored person. . . . [T]he only issue made [in this case] is as to the unconstitutionality of the act, so far as it requires the railway to provide separate accommodations, and the conductor to assign passengers according to their race.

It is claimed by [Plessy] that, in any mixed community, the reputation of belonging to the dominant race, in this instance the white race, is property, in the same sense that a right of action, or of inheritance, is *property.* Conceding this to be so, for the purposes of this case, we are unable to see how this statute deprives him of, or in any way affects his right to, such property. If he be a white man and assigned to a colored coach, he may have his action for damages against the company for being deprived of his so-called property. Upon the other hand, if he be a colored man and be so assigned, he has been deprived of no property, since he is not lawfully entitled to the reputation of being a white man.

In this connection it is also suggested that the same argument that will justify the state legislature in requiring railways to provide separate accommodations for the two races will also authorize them to require separate cars to be provided for people whose hair is of a certain color, or who are aliens, or who belong to certain nationalities, or to enact laws requiring colored people to walk upon one side of the street, and white people upon the other, or requiring white men's houses to be painted white, and colored men's black, or their vehicles or business signs to be of different colors, upon the theory that one side of the street is as good as the other, or that a house or vehicle of one color is as good as one of another color. The reply to all this is that every exercise of the police power must be reasonable, and extend only to such laws as are enacted in good faith for the promotion of the public good, and not

for the annoyance or oppression of a particular class.
Thus in *Yick Wo v. Hopkins*, it was held by this court
that a municipal ordinance of the city of San Francisco to
regulate the carrying on of public laundries within the
limits of the municipality violated the provisions of the
Constitution of the United States if it conferred upon the
municipal authorities arbitrary power, at their own will,
and without regard to discretion, in the legal sense of the
term, to give or withhold consent as to persons or places,
without regard to the competency of the persons applying,
or the propriety of the places selected for the carrying on
of the business. It was held to be a covert attempt on the
part of the municipality to make an arbitrary and unjust
discrimination against the Chinese race. While this was
the case of a municipal ordinance a like principle has been
held to apply to acts of a state legislature passed in the exercise of the police power.

So far, then, as a conflict with the 14th Amendment is
concerned, the case reduces itself to the question whether
the statute of Louisiana is a reasonable regulation, and
with respect to this there must necessarily be a large discretion on the part of the legislature. In determining the
question of reasonableness it is at liberty to act with reference to the established usages, customs, and traditions of
the people, and with a view to the promotion of their
comfort, and the preservation of the public peace and
good order. Gauged by this standard, we cannot say that a
law which authorizes or even requires the separation of
the two races in public conveyances is unreasonable or
more obnoxious to the 14th Amendment than the acts of
Congress requiring separate schools for colored children
in the District of Columbia, the constitutionality of which
does not seem to have been questioned, or the correspond-
ing acts of state legislatures.

We consider the underlying fallacy of [Plessy's] argument to consist in the assumption that the enforced separation of the two races stamps the colored race with a badge of inferiority. If this be so, it is not by reason of anything found in the act, but solely because the colored race chooses to put that construction upon it. The argument necessarily assumes that if, as has been more than once the case, and is not unlikely to be so again, the colored race should become the dominant power in the state legislature, and should enact a law in precisely similar terms, it would thereby relegate the white race to an inferior position. We imagine that the white race, at least, would not acquiesce in this assumption. The argument also assumes that social prejudices may be overcome by legislation, and that equal rights cannot be secured to the negro except by an enforced commingling of the two races. We cannot accept this proposition. If the two races are to meet on terms of social equality, it must be the result of natural affinities, a mutual appreciation of each other's merits and a voluntary consent of individuals. As was said by the court of appeals of New York in *People v. Gallagher*, "this end can neither be accomplished nor promoted by laws which conflict with the general sentiment of the community upon whom they are designed to operate. When the government, therefore, has secured to each of its citizens equal rights before the law and equal opportunities for improvement and progress, it has accomplished the end for which it is organized and performed all of the functions respecting social advantages with which it is endowed." Legislation is powerless to eradicate racial instincts or to abolish distinctions based upon physical differences, and the attempt to do so can only result in accentuating the difficulties of the present situation. If the civil and political rights of both races be equal, one cannot be inferior to the other civilly or politically. If one race be inferior to the other socially, the Constitution of the United States cannot put them upon the same plane.

It is true that the question of the proportion of colored blood necessary to constitute a colored person, as distinguished from a white person, is one upon which there is a difference of opinion in the different states, some holding that any visible admixture of black blood stamps the person as belonging to the colored race;others that it depends upon the preponderance of blood; and still others that the predominance of white blood must only be in the proportion of three fourths. But these are questions to be determined under the laws of each state and are not properly put in issue in this case. Under the allegation of his petition it may undoubtedly become a question of importance whether, under the laws of Louisiana, the petitioner belongs to the white or colored race.

The judgment of the court [below] is therefore affirmed.

JUSTICE HARLAN, dissenting: By the Louisiana statute, the validity of which is here involved, all railway companies (other than street railway companies) carrying passengers in that state are required to have separate but equal accommodations for white and colored persons, "by providing two or more passenger coaches for each passenger train, *or* by dividing the passenger coaches by *partition* so as to secure separate accommodations." Under this statute, no colored person is permitted to occupy a seat in a coach assigned to white persons; nor any white person to occupy a seat in the coach assigned to colored persons. The managers of the railroad are not allowed to exercise any discretion in the premises, but are required to assign each passenger to some coach or compartment set apart for the exclusive use of his race. If a passenger insists upon going into a coach or compartment not set apart for persons of his race, he is subject to be fined, or to be imprisoned in the parish jail. Penalties are prescribed for the refusal or neglect of the officers, directors, conductors, and employees of railroad companies to comply with the provisions of the act.

Only "nurses attending children of the other race" are excepted from the operation of the statute. No exception is made of colored attendants traveling with adults. A white man is not permitted to have his colored servant with him in the same coach, even if his condition of health requires the constant personal assistance of such servant. If a colored maid insists upon riding in the same coach with a white woman whom she has been employed to serve, and who may need her personal attention while traveling, she is subject to be fined or imprisoned for such an exhibition of zeal in the discharge of duty. While there may be in Louisiana persons of different races who are not citizens of the United States, the words in the act, "white and colored races" necessarily include all citizens of the United States of both races residing in that state. So that we have before us a state enactment that compels, under penalties, the separation of the two races in railroad passenger coaches, and makes it a crime for a citizen of either race to enter a coach that has been assigned to citizens of the other race.

Thus the state regulates the use of a public highway by citizens of the United States solely upon the basis of race.

However apparent the injustice of such legislation may be, we have only to consider whether it is consistent with the Constitution of the United States.

That a railroad is a public highway, and that the corporation which owns or operates it is in the exercise of public
functions, is not, at this day, to be disputed. . . . Very early the question arose whether a state's right of eminent
domain could be exercised by a private corporation created for the purpose of constructing a railroad. Clearly it
could not, unless taking land for such a purpose by such
an agency is taking land for public use. The right of eminent domain nowhere justifies taking property for a private use. Yet it is a doctrine universally accepted that a
state legislature may authorize a private corporation to
take land for the construction of such a road, making
compensation to the owner. What else does this doctrine
mean if not that building a railroad, though it be built by
a private corporation, is an act done for a public use?" So,
in *Pine Grove Twp. v. Talcott.* "Though the corporation [a
railroad company] was private, its work was public, as
much so as if it were to be constructed by the state." . . .

In respect of civil rights, common to all citizens, the Constitution of the United States does not, I think, permit any
public authority to know the race of those entitled to be
protected in the enjoyment of such rights. Every true
man has pride of race, and under appropriate circumstances, when the rights of others, his equals before the
law, are not to be affected, it is his privilege to express
such pride and to take such action based upon it as to him
seems proper. But I deny that any legislative body or judicial tribunal may have regard to the race of citizens
when the civil rights of those citizens are involved. Indeed such legislation as that here in question is inconsistent, not only with that equality of rights which pertains to
citizenship, national and state, but with the personal liberty enjoyed by every one within the United States.

The 13th Amendment does not permit the withholding or the deprivation of any right necessarily inhering in freedom. It not only struck down the institution of slavery as previously existing in the United States, but it prevents the imposition of any burdens or disabilities that constitute badges of slavery or servitude. It decreed universal civil freedom in this country. This court has so adjudged. But that amendment having been found inadequate to the protection of the rights of those who had been in slavery, it was followed by the 14th Amendment, which added greatly to the dignity and glory of American citizenship, and to the security of personal liberty, by declaring that "all persons born or naturalized in the United States, and subject to the jurisdiction thereof, are citizens of the United States and of the state wherein they reside," and that "no state shall make or enforce any law which shall abridge the privileges or immunities of citizens of the United States; nor shall any state deprive any person of life, liberty, or property without due process of law, nor deny to any person within its jurisdiction the equal protection of the laws." These two amendments, if enforced according to their true intent and meaning, will protect all the civil rights that pertain to freedom and citizenship. Finally, and to the end that no citizen should be denied, on account of his race, the privilege of participating in the political control of his country, it was declared by the 15th Amendment that "the right of citizens of the United States to vote shall not be denied or abridged by the United States or by any state on account of race, color, or previous condition of servitude."

These notable additions to the fundamental law were welcomed by the friends of liberty throughout the world. They removed the race line from our governmental systems. They had, as this court has said, a common purpose,

namely, to secure "to a race recently emancipated, a race
that through many generations have been held in slavery,
all the civil rights that the superior race enjoy." They declared, in legal effect, this court has further said, "that the
law in the states shall be the same for the black as for the
white; that all persons, whether colored or white, shall
stand equal before the laws of the states, and, in regard to
the colored race, for whose protection the amendment was
primarily designed, that no discrimination shall be made
against them by law because of their color." We also said:
"The words of the amendment, it is true, are prohibitory,
but they contain a necessary implication of a positive immunity, or right, most valuable to the colored race - the
right to exemption from unfriendly legislation against
them distinctively as colored - exemption from legal discriminations, implying inferiority in civil society, lessen-
ing the security of their enjoyment of the rights which
others enjoy, and discriminations which are steps towards
reducing them to the condition of a subject race." It was
consequently adjudged that a state law that excluded citizens of the colored race from juries because of their race
and however well qualified in other respects to discharge
the duties of jurymen was repugnant to the 14th Amendment. At the present term, . . . this court declared that
"underlying all of those decisions is the principle that the
constitution of the United States, in its present form, forbids, so far as civil and political rights are concerned, discrimination by the general government or the states
against any citizen because of his race. All citizens are
equal before the law."

The decisions referred to show the scope of the recent
amendments of the Constitution. They also show that it is
not within the power of a state to prohibit colored citi-

zens, because of their race, from participating as jurors in the administration of justice.

It was said in argument that the statute of Louisiana does not discriminate against either race, but prescribes a rule applicable alike to white and colored citizens. But this argument does not meet the difficulty. Everyone knows that the statute in question had its origin in the purpose, not so much to exclude white persons from railroad cars occupied by blacks, as to exclude colored people from coaches occupied by or assigned to white persons. Railroad corporations of Louisiana did not make discrimination among whites in the matter of accommodation for travelers. The thing to accomplish was, under the guise of giving equal accommodation for whites and blacks to compel the latter to keep to themselves while traveling in railroad passenger coaches. No one would be so wanting in candor as to assert the contrary. The fundamental objection, therefore, to the statute, is that it interferes with the personal freedom of citizens. "Personal liberty," it has been well said, "consists in the power of locomotion, of changing situation, or removing one's person to whatsoever places one's own inclination may direct, without imprisonment or restraint, unless by due course of law." If a white man and a black man choose to occupy the same public conveyance on a public highway, it is their right to do so, and no government, proceeding alone on grounds of race, can prevent it without infringing the personal liberty of each.

It is one thing for railroad carriers to furnish, or to be required by law to furnish, equal accommodations for all whom they are under a legal duty to carry. It is quite another thing for government to forbid citizens of the white and black races from traveling in the same public

conveyance, and to punish officers of railroad companies
for permitting persons of the two races to occupy the
same passenger coach. If a state can prescribe as a rule of
civil conduct, that whites and blacks shall not travel as
passengers in the same railroad coach, why may it not so
regulate the use of the streets of its cities and towns as to
compel white citizens to keep on one side of the street
and black citizens to keep on the other? Why may it not,
upon like grounds, punish whites and blacks who ride together in street cars or in open vehicles on a public road
or street? Why may it not require sheriffs to assign
whites to one side of a courtroom and blacks to the other?
And why may it not also prohibit the commingling of the
two races in the galleries of legislative halls or in public
assemblages convened for the political questions of the
day? Further, if this statute of Louisiana is consistent
with the personal liberty of citizens, why may not the
state require the separation in railroad coaches of native
and naturalized citizens of the United States, or of Protes-
tants and Roman Catholics?

The answer given at the argument to these questions was
that regulations of the kind they suggest would be unreasonable, and could not, therefore, stand before the law. It
is meant that the determination of questions of legislative
power depends upon the inquiry whether the statute
whose validity is questioned is, in the judgment of the
courts, a reasonable one, taking all the circumstances into
consideration? A statute may be unreasonable merely because a sound public policy forbade its enactment. But I
do not understand that the courts have anything to do
with the policy or expediency of legislation. A statute
may be valid, and yet upon grounds of public policy may
well be characterized as unreasonable. Mr. Sedgwick correctly states the rule when he says that the legislative in-

tention being clearly ascertained, "the courts have no other duty to perform than to execute the legislative will, without any regard to their views as to the wisdom or justice of the particular enactment." There is a dangerous tendency in these latter days to enlarge the functions of the courts, by means of judicial interference with the will of the people as expressed by the legislature. Our institutions have the distinguishing characteristic that the three departments of government are coordinate and separate. Each must keep within the limits defined by the Constitution. And the courts best discharge their duty by executing the will of the lawmaking power, constitutionally expressed, leaving the results of legislation to be dealt with by the people through their representatives. Statutes must always have a reasonable construction. Sometimes they are to be construed strictly; sometimes literally, in order to carry out the legislative will. But however construed, the intent of the legislature is to be respected, if the particular statute in question is valid, although the courts, looking at the public interests, may conceive the statute to be both unreasonable and impolitic. If the power exists to enact a statute, that ends the matter so far as the courts are concerned. The adjudged cases in which statutes have been held to be void, because unreasonable, are those in which the means employed by the legislature were not at all germane to the end to which the legislature was competent.

The white race deems itself to be the dominant race in this country. And so it is, in prestige, in achievements, in education, in wealth, and in power. So, I doubt not that it will continue to be for all time, if it remains true to its great heritage and holds fast to the principles of constitutional liberty. But in view of the Constitution, in the eye of the law, there is in this country no superior, dominant, ruling class of citizens. There is no caste here. Our Constitution is color-blind, and neither knows nor tolerates classes among citizens. In respect of civil rights, all citizens are equal before the law. The humblest is the peer of the most powerful. The law regards man as man, and takes no account of his surroundings or of his color when his civil rights as guaranteed by the supreme law of the land are involved. It is therefore to be regretted that this high tribunal, the final expositor of the fundamental law of the land, has reached the conclusion that it is competent for a state to regulate the enjoyment by citizens of their civil rights solely upon the basis of race.

In my opinion, the judgment this day rendered will, in time, prove to be quite as pernicious as the decision made by this tribunal in the *Dred Scott Case.* It was adjudged in that case that the descendants of Africans who were imported into this country and sold as slaves were not included nor intended to be included under the word "citizens" in the Constitution, and could not claim any of the rights and privileges which that instrument provided for and secured to citizens of the United States; that at the time of the adoption of the Constitution they were "considered as a subordinate and inferior class of beings, who had been subjugated by the dominant race, and, whether emancipated or not, yet remained subject to their authority, and had no rights or privileges but such as those who held the power and the government might choose to grant them." The recent amendments of the Constitution, it was supposed, had eradicated these principles from our institutions. But it seems that we have yet, in some of the states, a dominant race, a superior class of citizens, which assumes to regulate the enjoyment of civil rights, common to all citizens, upon the basis of race. The present decision, it may well be apprehended, will not stimulate aggressions, more or less brutal and irritating, upon the admitted rights of colored citizens, but will encourage the belief that it is possible, by means of state enactments, to defeat the beneficent purposes which the people of the United States had in view when they adopted the recent amendments of the Constitution, by one of which the blacks of this country were made citizens of the United States and of the states in which they respectively reside and whose privileges and immunities, as citizens, the states are forbidden to abridge. Sixty millions of whites are in no danger from the presence here of eight millions of blacks. The destinies of the two races in this country are indissolubly linked together, and the interests of both require that the common government of all shall not permit the seeds of race hate to be planted under the sanction of law. What can more certainly arouse race hate, what more certainly create and perpetuate a feeling of distrust between these races, than state enactments which in fact proceed on the ground that colored citizens are so inferior and degraded that they cannot be allowed to sit in public coaches occupied by white citizens? That, as all will admit, is the real meaning of such legislation as was enacted in Louisiana.

The sure guaranty of the peace and security of each race is the clear, distinct, unconditional recognition by our governments, national and state, of every right that inheres in civil freedom, and of the equality before the law of all citizens of the United States without regard to race. State enactments, regulating the enjoyment of civil rights, upon the basis of race, and cunningly devised to defeat legitimate results of the [Civil W]ar, under the pretense of recognizing equality of rights, can have no other result than to render permanent peace impossible and to keep alive a conflict of races, the continuance of which must do harm to all concerned. This question is not met by the suggestion that social equality cannot exist between the white and black races in this country. That argument, if it can be properly regarded as one, is scarcely worthy of consideration, for social equality no more exists between two races when traveling in a passenger coach or a public highway than when members of the same races sit by each other in a street car or in the jury box, or stand or sit with each other in a political assembly, or when they use in common the streets of a city or town, or when they are in the same room for the purpose of having their names placed on the registry of voters, or when they approach the ballot-box in order to exercise the high privilege of voting.

There is a race so different from our own that we do not permit those belonging to it to become citizens of the United States. Persons belonging to it are, with few exceptions, absolutely excluded from our country. I allude to the Chinese race. But by the statute in question a Chinaman can ride in the same passenger coach with white citizens of the United States, while citizens of the black race in Louisiana, many of whom, perhaps, risked their lives for the preservation of the Union, who are entitled by law to participate in the political control of the state and nation, who are not excluded, by law or by reason of their race, from public stations of any kind, and who have all the legal rights that belong to white citizens, are yet declared to be criminals, liable to imprisonment, if they ride in a public coach occupied by citizens of the white race. It is scarcely just to say that a colored citizen should not object to occupying a public coach assigned to his own race. He does not object, nor, perhaps, would he object to separate coaches for his race, if his rights under the law were recognized. But he does object, and he ought never to cease objecting, that citizens of the white and black races can be adjudged criminals because they sit, or claim the right to sit, in the same public coach on a public highway.

The arbitrary separation of citizens, on the basis of race, while they are on a public highway, is a badge of servitude wholly inconsistent with the civil freedom and the equality before the law established by the Constitution. It cannot be justified upon any legal grounds.

If evils will result from the commingling of the two races upon public highways established for the benefit of all, they will be infinitely less than those that will surely come from state legislation regulating the enjoyment of civil rights upon the basis of race. We boast of the freedom enjoyed by our people above all other peoples. But it is difficult to reconcile that boast with a state of the law which, practically, puts the brand of servitude and degradation upon a large class of our fellow citizens, our equals before the law. The thin disguise of "equal" accommodations for passengers in railroad coaches will not mislead anyone, or atone for the wrong this day done.

The result of the whole matter is that while this court has frequently adjudged, and at the present term has recognized the doctrine, that a state cannot, consistently with the Constitution of the United States, prevent white and black citizens, having the required qualifications for jury service, from sitting in the same jury box, it is now solemnly held that a state may prohibit white and black citizens from sitting in the same passenger coach on a public highway, or may require that they be separated by a "partition" when in the same passenger coach. May it not now be reasonably expected that astute men of the domi-

nant race, who affect to be disturbed at the possibility
that the integrity of the white race may be corrupted, or
that its supremacy will be imperiled, by contact on public
highways with black people, will endeavor to procure statutes requiring white and black jurors to be separated in
the jury box by a "partition," and that, upon retiring from
the court room to consult as to their verdict, such partition, if it be a movable one, shall be taken to their consul-
tation room, and set up in such way as to prevent black
jurors from coming too close to their brother jurors of the
white race. If the "partition" used in the court room hap-
pens to be stationary, provision could be made for screens
with openings through which jurors of the two races
could confer as to their verdict without coming into personal contact with each other. I cannot see but that, according to the principles this day announced, such state
legislation, although conceived in hostility to, and enacted
for the purpose of humiliating, citizens of the United
States of a particular race, would be held to be consistent
with the Constitution.

I do not deem it necessary to review the decisions of state
courts to which reference was made in argument. Some,
and the most important, of them are wholly inapplicable,
because rendered prior to the adoption of the last amendments of the Constitution, when colored people had very
few rights which the dominant race felt obliged to respect. Others were made at a time when public opinion,
in many localities, was dominated by the institution of
slavery; when it would not have been safe to do justice to
the black man; and when, so far as the rights of blacks
were concerned, race prejudice was, practically, the supreme law of the land. Those decisions cannot be guides
in the era introduced by the recent amendments of the supreme law, which established universal civil freedom, gave

citizenship to all born or naturalized in the United States and residing here, obliterated the race line from our systems of governments, national and state, and placed our free institutions upon the broad and sure foundation of the equality of all men before the law.

I am of opinion that the statute of Louisiana is inconsistent with the personal liberty of citizens, white and black, in that state, and hostile to both the spirit and letter of the Constitution of the United States. If laws of like character should be enacted in the several states of the Union, the effect would be in the highest degree mischievous. Slavery as an institution tolerated by law would, it is true, have disappeared from our country, but there would remain a power in the states, by sinister legislation, to interfere with the full enjoyment of the blessings of freedom; to regulate civil rights, common to all citizens, upon the basis of race; and to place in a condition of legal inferiority a large body of American citizens, now constituting a part of the political community, called the people of the United States, for whom and by whom, through representatives, our government is administered. Such a system is inconsistent with the guarantee given by the Constitution to each state of a republican form of government, and may be stricken down by congressional action, or by the courts in the discharge of their solemn duty to maintain the supreme law of the land, anything in the Constitution or laws of any state to the contrary notwithstanding.

For the reasons stated, I am constrained to withhold my assent from the opinion and judgment of the majority.

The Separate But Equal Doctrine established by the United States Supreme Court in Plessy v. Ferguson *was not overturned by the Court until their landmark 1954 School Desegregation decision in* Brown v. The Board of Education of Topeka, Kansas.

TRUST BUSTING

Standard Oil v. The United States

Every person who shall monopolize, or attempt to monopolize, or combine or conspire with any other person to monopolize any part of the trade or commerce among the several states ... shall be guilty of a misdemeanor.

The Sherman Anti-Trust Act

In 1870 John Davidson Rockefeller and others organized Standard Oil of Ohio. By 1882 Standard Oil controlled the oil fields, pipelines, and refineries of Ohio, New York, and Pennsylvania. The Standard Oil monopoly was able to fix prices, limit production, and control transportation of oil and oil products. In 1882 other competing oil companies began to join the monopoly by placing their stock in the Rockefeller-controlled Standard Oil Trust. The Trust grew to control over eighty oil-related companies. On March 2, 1892 the Ohio Supreme Court found the Standard Oil Trust in violation of Ohio's anti-trust laws and ordered it dissolved. To avoid the Ohio dissolution order, Standard Oil of New Jersey, a company controlled by the Rockefeller interests, was created and the Trust transferred its oil company stock into it.

On November 15, 1906 the United States charged Standard Oil of New Jersey, John D. Rockefeller, and others, with violations of the Sherman Anti-Trust Act. Passed by the Congress on July 2, 1890 the Sherman Anti-Trust Act made interstate monopolies of entire industries illegal. A Federal Court found Standard Oil of New Jersey to be in violation of the Sherman Act and ordered Rockefeller to dissolve his oil monopoly into independent competing corporations. Standard Oil and Rockefeller appealed to the United States Supreme Court.

Oral arguments commenced on March 14, 1910. On May 15, 1911 Chief Justice Edward Douglas White announced the decision of the Court. The edited text follows.

THE STANDARD OIL COURT

Chief Justice Edward Douglas White
Appointed by President Cleveland
Served 1894 - 1921

Associate Justice John Marshall Harlan
Appointed by President Hayes
Served 1877 -1911

Associate Justice Joseph McKenna
Appointed by President McKinley
Served 1898 - 1925

Associate Justice Oliver Wendell Holmes, Jr.
Appointed by President Theodore Roosevelt
Served 1902 - 1932

Associate Justice William R. Day
Appointed by President Theodore Roosevelt
Served 1903 - 1922

Associate Justice Horace H. Lurton
Appointed by President Taft
Served 1909 - 1914

Associate Justice Charles Evans Hughes
Appointed Associate Justice by President Taft
Appointed Chief Justice by President Hoover
Served 1910 - 1916, 1930 - 1941

Associate Justice Willis Van Devanter
Appointed by President Taft
Served 1910 - 1937

Associate Justice Joseph R. Lamar
Appointed by President Taft
Served 1910 - 1916

The full text of *Standard Oil v. United States* can be found on page 1, volume 221 of *United States Reports.*

STANDARD OIL v. UNITED STATES
MAY 15, 1911

CHIEF JUSTICE WHITE: The Standard Oil Company of New Jersey and thirty-three other corporations, John D. Rockefeller, William Rockefeller, and five other individual defendants, prosecute this appeal to reverse a decree of the court below [the Circuit Court for the Eastern District of Missouri]. . . .

[It was charged] that the various defendants were engaged in conspiring "to restrain the trade and commerce in petroleum, commonly called 'crude oil,' in refined oil, and in the other products of petroleum, among the several states and territories of the United States and the District of Columbia and with foreign nations, and to monopolize the said commerce." The conspiracy was alleged to have been formed in or about the year 1870 by three of the individual defendants: John D. Rockefeller, William Rockefeller, and Henry M. Flagler. . . .

The general charge concerning the period from 1870 to 1882 was as follows:

"That during said first period the said individual defendants, in connection with the Standard Oil Company of Ohio, purchased and obtained interests through stock ownership and otherwise in, and entered into agreements with, various persons, firms, corporations, and limited partnerships engaged in purchasing, shipping, refining, and selling petroleum and its products among the various states, for the purpose of fixing the price of crude and refined oil and the products thereof, limiting the production thereof, and controlling the transportation therein, and thereby restraining trade and commerce among the several states, and monopolizing the said commerce."

. . . . [It was also charged] that both the Standard Oil Trust from 1882 to 1899, and the Standard Oil Company of New Jersey, since 1899, had monopolized and restrained interstate commerce in petroleum and its products. . . [by r]ebates, preferences, and other discriminatory practices in favor of the combination by railroad companies; restraint and monopolization by control of pipelines, and unfair practices against competing pipe lines; contracts with competitors in restraint of trade; unfair methods of competition, such as local price cutting at the points where necessary to suppress competition; espionage of the business of competitors, the operation of bogus independent companies, and payment of rebates on oil, with the like intent; the division of the United States into districts, and the limiting the operations of the various subsidiary corporations as to such districts so that competition in the sale of petroleum products between such corporations had been entirely eliminated and destroyed; and finally reference was made to what was alleged to be the "enormous and unreasonable profits" earned by the Standard Oil Trust and the Standard Oil Company as a result of the alleged monopoly. . . .

The court decided in favor of the United States. In the opinion delivered, all the multitude of acts of wrongdoing charged in the bill were put aside, in so far as they were alleged to have been committed prior to the passage of the anti-trust act, "except as evidence of their (the defendants') purpose, of their continuing conduct, and of its effect."

... [I]t was adjudged that the combining of the stocks of various companies in the hands of the Standard Oil Company of New Jersey in 1899 constituted a combination in restraint of trade and also an attempt to monopolize and a monopolization under Section 2 of the anti-trust act. The decree was against seven individual defendants, the Standard Oil Company of New Jersey, thirty-six domestic companies, and one foreign company which the Standard Oil Company of New Jersey controls by stock ownership; these thirty-eight corporate defendants being held to be parties to the combination found to exist.

... The Standard Oil Company of New Jersey was enjoined [stopped] from voting the stocks or exerting any control over the said thirty-seven subsidiary companies, and the subsidiary companies were enjoined from paying any dividends as to the Standard Company, or permitting it to exercise any control over them by virtue of the stock ownership or power acquired by means of the combination. The individuals and corporations were also enjoined from entering into or carrying into effect any like combination which would evade the decree. Further, the individual defendants, the Standard Company, and the thirty-seven subsidiary corporations, were enjoined from engaging or continuing in interstate commerce in petroleum or its products during the continuance of the illegal combination.

[T]o discover and state the truth concerning these contentions both arguments call for the analysis and weighing ... of a jungle of conflicting testimony covering a period of forty years. ...

We quote the text of the 1st and 2d sections of the [Anti-Trust A]ct, as follows:

"Section 1. Every contract, combination in the form of trust or otherwise, or conspiracy, in restraint of trade or commerce among the several states or with foreign nations, is hereby declared to be illegal. Every person who shall make any such contract, or engage in any such combination or conspiracy, shall be deemed guilty of a misdemeanor, and, on conviction thereof, shall be punished by fine not exceeding $5,000, or by imprisonment not exceeding one year, or by both said punishments, in the discretion of the court.

"Sec. 2. Every person who shall monopolize, or attempt to monopolize, or combine or conspire with any other person or persons to monopolize, any part of the trade or commerce among the several states, or with foreign nations, shall be deemed guilty of a misdemeanor, and, on conviction thereof, shall be punished by fine not exceeding $5,000, or by imprisonment not exceeding one year, or by both said punishments, in the discretion of the court."

. . . [A]lthough the statute, by the comprehensiveness of the enumerations embodied in both the 1st and 2d sections, makes it certain that its purpose was to prevent undue restraints of every kind or nature, nevertheless by the omission of any direct prohibition against monopoly in the concrete, it indicates a consciousness that the freedom of the individual right to contract, when not unduly or improperly exercised, was the most efficient means for the prevention of monopoly. . . . [F]reedom to contract was the essence of freedom from undue restraint on the right to contract. . . .

... [T]he court below held that the acts and dealings established by the proof operated to destroy the "potentiality of competition" which otherwise would have existed to such an extent as to cause the transfers of stock which were made to the New Jersey Corporation and the control which resulted over the many and various subsidiary corporations to be a combination or conspiracy in restraint of trade, in violation of the 1st section of the act, but also to be an attempt to monopolize and monopolization bringing about a perennial violation of the 2d section.

We see no cause to doubt the correctness of these conclusions. . . .

We think no disinterested mind can survey the period in question without being irresistibly driven to the conclusion that the very genius for commercial development and organization which it would seem was manifested from the beginning soon begot an intent and purpose to exclude others which was frequently manifested by acts and dealings wholly inconsistent with the theory that they were made with the single conception of advancing the development of business power by usual methods, but which, on the contrary, necessarily involved the intent to drive others from the field and to exclude them from their right to trade, and thus accomplish the mastery which was the end in view. And, considering the period from the date of the trust agreements of 1879 and 1882, up to the time of the expansion of the New Jersey corporation, the gradual extension of the power over the commerce in oil which ensued, the decision of the supreme court of Ohio, the tardiness or reluctance in conforming to the commands of that decision, the methods first adopted and that which finally culminated in the plan of the New Jersey corporation, all additionally serve to make manifest the

continued existence of the intent which we have previously indicated, and which, among other things, impelled the
expansion of the New Jersey corporation. The exercise of
the power which resulted from that organization fortifies
the foregoing conclusions, since the development which
came, the acquisition here and there which ensued of every efficient means by which competition could have been
asserted, the slow but resistless methods which followed
by which means of transportation were absorbed and
brought under control, the system of marketing which was
adopted by which the country was divided into districts
and the trade in each district in oil was turned over to a
designated corporation within the combination, and all
others were excluded, all lead the mind up to a conviction
of a purpose and intent which we think is so certain as
practically to cause the subject not to be within the domain of reasonable contention.

The inference that no attempt to monopolize could have
been intended, and that no monopolization resulted from
the acts complained of, since it is established that a very
small percentage of the crude oil produced was controlled
by the combination, is unwarranted. As substantial power
over the crude product was the inevitable result of the absolute control which existed over the refined product, the
monopolization of the one carried with it the power to
control the other; and if the inferences which this situation suggests were developed, . . . they might well serve to
add additional cogency to the presumption of intent to
monopolize which we have found arises from the unquestioned proof on other subjects.

. . . So far as the decree [of the lower court] held that the
ownership of the stock of the New Jersey corporation

constituted a combination in violation of the 1st section and an attempt to create a monopoly or to monopolize under the 2d section, and commanded the dissolution of the combination, the decree was clearly appropriate. . . .

Our conclusion is that the decree below was right and should be affirmed [upheld].

CHILD LABOR

Hammer v. Dagenhart

No product of any mill, cannery, workshop, factory or manufactory situated in the United States shall be shipped or delivered interstate in which children under the age of fourteen have been permitted to work or children between the ages of fourteen years and sixteen years have been permitted to work more than eight hours any day or for more than six days in any week or after the hour of 7 PM or before the hour of 6 AM.

The Keating-Owen Child Labor Law

On September 1, 1916 the U.S. Congress enacted the first Federal Child Labor Law. Under the authority of the Constitution's Commerce Clause, the interstate commerce of the products of child labor was prohibited.

Roland Dagenhart had two children, John, then under the age of fourteen, and Reuben, then under the age of sixteen. Both worked in a Charlotte, North Carolina cotton mill. The enforcement of the Federal Child Labor Law would, Roland Dagenhart stated, drastically reduce his family income. John's job would be lost, Reuben's hours would be cut. Dagenhart, on his own behalf and on behalf of his underage sons, sued W.C. Hammer, the U.S. District Attorney in North Carolina, to halt the enforcement of the law. Dagenhart's lawyers argued that under the Tenth Amendment the power to regulate child labor belonged not to the federal government but to the states. The U.S. District Court for North Carolina found the Federal Child Labor Law unconstitutional. Hammer appealed to the United States Supreme Court.

Oral arguments commenced on April 15, 1918. On June 3, 1918 Justice William Rufus Day announced the 5-4 decision. The edited text follows.

THE DAGENHART COURT

Chief Justice Edward Douglas White
Appointed by President Cleveland
Served 1894 - 1921

Associate Justice Joseph McKenna
Appointed by President McKinley
Served 1898 - 1925

Associate Justice Oliver Wendell Holmes, Jr.
Appointed by President Theodore Roosevelt
Served 1902 - 1932

Associate Justice William R. Day
Appointed by President Theodore Roosevelt
Served 1903 - 1922

Associate Justice Willis Van Devanter
Appointed by President Taft
Served 1910 - 1937

Associate Justice Mahlon Pitney
Appointed by President Taft
Served 1912 -1922

Associate Justice James McReynolds
Appointed by President Wilson
Served 1914 -1941

Associate Justice Louis D. Brandeis
Appointed by President Wilson
Served 1916 - 1939

Associate Justice John H. Clarke
Appointed by President Wilson
Served 1916 - 1922

The unedited text of *Hammer v. Dagenhart* can be found
on page 251, volume 247, of *United States Reports.*

W.C. HAMMER v.
ROLAND H. DAGENHART
JUNE 3, 1918

JUSTICE DAY: A bill was filed in the United States district court for the western district of North Carolina by a father in his own behalf and as next friend of his two minor sons, one under the age of fourteen years and the other between the ages of fourteen and sixteen years, employees in a cotton mill at Charlotte, North Carolina, to enjoin [stop] the enforcement of the act of Congress intended to prevent interstate commerce in the products of child labor.

The district court held the act unconstitutional and entered a decree [order] enjoining its enforcement. This appeal brings the case here. . . .

The attack upon the act rests upon three propositions: First. It is not a regulation of interstate and foreign commerce. Second. It contravenes [contradicts] the Tenth Amendment to the Constitution. Third. It conflicts with the Fifth Amendment to the Constitution.

The controlling question for decision is: Is it within the authority of Congress in regulating commerce among the states to prohibit the transportation in interstate commerce of manufactured goods, the product of a factory in which, within thirty days prior to their removal therefrom, children under the age of fourteen have been employed or permitted to work, or children between the ages of fourteen and sixteen years have been employed or permitted to work, more than eight hours in any day, or more than six days in any week, or after the hour of 7 o'clock P.M. or before the hour of 6 o'clock A.M.?

The power essential to the passage of this act, the government contends, is found in the commerce clause of the Constitution, which authorizes Congress to regulate commerce with foreign nations and among the states.

In *Gibbons v. Ogden*, Chief Justice Marshall, speaking for this court, and defining the extent and nature of the commerce power, said: "It is the power to regulate, that is, to prescribe the rule by which commerce is to be governed." In other words, the power is one to control the means by which commerce is carried on, which is directly the contrary of the assumed right to forbid commerce from moving and thus destroy it as to particular commodities. . . .

Champion v. Ames, the so-called Lottery Case, . . . held that Congress might pass a law having the effect to keep the channels of commerce free from use in the transportation of tickets used in the promotion of lottery schemes. In *Hipolite Egg Co. v. United States*, this court sustained [maintained] the power of Congress to pass the Pure Food and Drug Act, which prohibited the introduction into the states by means of interstate commerce of impure foods and drugs. In *Hoke v. United States*, this court sustained the constitutionality of the so-called "White Slave Traffic Act," whereby transportation of a woman in interstate commerce for the purpose of prostitution was forbidden. In that case we said, having reference to the authority of Congress, under the regulatory power, to protect the channels of interstate commerce:

"If the facility of interstate transportation can be taken away from the demoralization of lotteries, the debasement of obscene literature, the contagion of diseased cattle or persons, the impurity of food and drugs, the like facility can be taken away from the systematic enticement to and the enslavement in prostitution and debauchery of women, and, more insistently, of girls."

In *Caminetti v. United States*, we held that Congress might prohibit the transportation of women in interstate commerce for the purposes of debauchery and kindred purposes. In *Clark Distilling Co. v. Western Maryland*, the power of Congress over the transportation of intoxicating liquors was sustained. In the course of the opinion it was said:

"The power conferred is to regulate, and the very terms of the grant would seem to repel the contention that only prohibition of movement in interstate commerce was embraced. And the cogency of this is manifest since, if the doctrine were applied to those manifold and important subjects of interstate commerce as to which Congress from the beginning has regulated, not prohibited, the existence of government under the Constitution would be no longer possible."

And concluding the discussion which sustained the authority of the government to prohibit the transportation of liquor in interstate commerce, the court said:

"The exceptional nature of the subject here regulated is the basis upon which the exceptional power exerted must rest, and affords no ground for any fear that such power may be constitutionally extended to things which it may not, consistently with the guaranties of the Constitution, embrace."

In each of these instances the use of interstate transportation was necessary to the accomplishment of harmful results. In other words, although the power over interstate transportation was to regulate, that could only be accomplished by prohibiting the use of the facilities of interstate commerce to effect the evil intended.

This element is wanting in the present case. The thing intended to be accomplished by this statute is the denial of the facilities of interstate commerce to those manufacturers in the states who employ children within the prohibited ages. The act in its effect does not regulate transportation among the states, but aims to standardize the ages at which children may be employed in mining and manufacturing within the states. The goods shipped are of themselves harmless. The act permits them to be freely shipped after thirty days from the time of their removal from the factory. When offered for shipment, and before transportation begins, the labor of their production is over, and the mere fact that they were intended for interstate commerce transportation does not make their production subject to Federal control under the commerce power.

Commerce "consists of intercourse and traffic . . . and includes the transportation of persons and property, as well as the purchase, sale and exchange of commodities." The making of goods and the mining of coal are not commerce, nor does the fact that these things are to be afterwards shipped, or used in interstate commerce, make their production a part thereof.

Over interstate transportation, or its incidents, the regulatory power of Congress is ample, but the production of articles intended for interstate commerce is a matter of local regulation. "When the commerce begins is determined not by the character of the commodity, nor by the intention of the owner to transfer it to another state for sale, nor by his preparation of it for transportation, but by its actual delivery to a common carrier for transportation, or the actual commencement of its transfer to another state." This principle has been recognized often in this court. If it were otherwise, all manufacture intended for interstate shipment would be brought under Federal control to the practical exclusion of the authority of the states, a result certainly not contemplated by the framers of the Constitution when they vested in Congress the authority to regulate commerce among the states.

It is further contended that the authority of Congress may be exerted to control interstate commerce in the shipment of child-made goods because of the effect of the circulation of such goods in other states where the evil of this class of labor has been recognized by local legislation, and the right to thus employ child labor has been more rigorously restrained than in the state of production. In other words, that the unfair competition thus engendered may be controlled by closing the channels of interstate commerce to manufacturers in those states where the local laws do not meet what Congress deems to be the more just standard of other states.

There is no power vested in Congress to require the states to exercise their police power so as to prevent possible unfair competition. Many causes may cooperate to give one state, by reason of local laws or conditions, an economic advantage over others. The commerce clause was not intended to give to Congress a general authority to equalize such conditions. In some of the states laws have been passed fixing minimum wages for women; in others the local law regulates the hours of labor of women in various employments. Business done in such states may be at an economic disadvantage when compared with states which

have no such regulations; surely, this fact does not give
Congress the power to deny transportation in interstate
commerce to those who carry on business where the hours
of labor and the rate of compensation for women have
not been fixed by a standard in the use in other states and
approved by Congress.

The grant of power to Congress over the subject of interstate commerce was to enable it to regulate such commerce, and not to give it authority to control the states in
their exercise of the police power over local trade and
manufacture.

The grant of authority over a purely Federal matter was
not intended to destroy the local power always existing
and carefully reserved to the states in the 10th Amendment to the Constitution.

. . . . That there should be limitations upon the right to
employ children in mines and factories in the interest of
their own and the public welfare, all will admit.   That
such employment is generally deemed to require regulation is shown by the fact . . . that every state in the Union
has a law upon the subject, limiting the right to thus employ children.   In North Carolina, the state wherein is located the factory in which the employment was had in the
present case, no child under twelve years of age is permitted to work.

It may be desirable that such laws be uniform, but our
Federal government is one of enumerated powers; "this
principle," declared Chief Justice Marshall in *McCulloch
v. Maryland,* "is universally admitted."

A statute must be judged by its natural and reasonable effect. The control by Congress over interstate commerce cannot authorize the exercise of authority not intrusted to it by the Constitution. The maintenance of the authority of the states over matters purely local is as essential to the preservation of our institutions as is the conservation of the supremacy of the Federal power in all matters intrusted to the nation by the Federal Constitution.

In interpreting the Constitution it must never be forgotten that the nation is made up of states, to which are intrusted the powers of local government. And to them and to the people the powers not expressly delegated to the national government are reserved. The power of the states to regulate their purely internal affairs by such laws as seem wise to the local authority is inherent, and has never been surrendered to the general government. To sustain this statute would not be, in our judgment, a recognition of the lawful exertion of congressional authority over interstate commerce, but would sanction an invasion by the Federal power of the control of a matter purely local in its character, and over which no authority has been delegated to Congress in conferring the power to regulate commerce among the states.

We have neither authority nor disposition to question the motives of Congress in enacting this legislation. The purposes intended must be attained consistently with constitutional limitations, and not by an invasion of the powers of the states. This court has no more important function than that which devolves upon it the obligation to preserve inviolate the constitutional limitations upon the exercise of authority, Federal and state, to the end that each may continue to discharge, harmoniously with the other, the duties intrusted to it by the Constitution.

In our view the necessary effect of this act is, by means of a prohibition against the movement in interstate commerce of ordinary commercial commodities, to regulate the hours of labor of children in factories and mines within the states, a purely state authority. Thus the act in a twofold sense is repugnant to the Constitution. It not only transcends the authority delegated to Congress over commerce, but also exerts a power as to a purely local matter to which the Federal authority does not extend. The far-reaching result of upholding the act cannot be more plainly indicated than by pointing out that if Congress can thus regulate matters intrusted to local authority by prohibition of the movement of commodities in interstate commerce, all freedom of commerce will be at an end, and the power of the states over local matters may be eliminated, and thus our system of government be practically destroyed.

For these reasons we hold that this law exceeds the constitutional authority of Congress. It follows that the decree of the District Court must be affirmed [upheld].

In 1919 the Congress enacted the Child Labor Tax Act, which added a federal excise tax to the products of child labor, making them less competitive. In 1922 the Supreme Court found the Child Labor Tax Act unconstitutional. In 1924 the Congress proposed to the states the Child Labor Amendment to the United States Constitution, which would have prohibited the use of child labor. The Child Labor Amendment failed to win ratification by the required two-thirds of the states. In 1938 the Congress enacted the Fair Labor Standards Act, which, among other provisions, prohibited the use of child labor. In 1941 the Supreme Court upheld the constitutionality of this Act and prohibited the use of child labor.

THE ATOMIC SPIES

Julius and Ethel Rosenberg v. United States

Whoever, with intent or reason to believe that it is to be used to the injury of the United States or to the advantage of a foreign nation, delivers to any foreign government any information relating to the national defense in time of war shall be punished by death or imprisonment.

The Espionage Act of 1917

On April 5, 1951 Julius and Ethel Rosenberg were found guilty of espionage against the United States in time of war. In an unprecedented action, Judge Irving Kaufman sentenced the Rosenbergs to death. No federal court had ever before imposed the death penalty in an espionage case. Judge Kaufman wrote: "I feel I must [impose the death] sentence upon the [Rosenbergs] in this diabolical conspiracy to destroy a God-fearing nation." The "diabolical conspiracy" was the 1944 theft, from Los Alamos National Laboratory, of the secrets to the American atomic bomb, which the Rosenbergs, and others, gave to the Soviet Union. Indicted on August 17, 1950, the Rosenbergs were tried and convicted for wartime crimes under the Espionage Act of 1917. Over the next 26 months the Rosenbergs appealed their death sentences to the U.S. Court of Appeals and the U.S. Supreme Court.

On June 15, 1953 the Supreme Court denied their sixth appeal. Their execution was scheduled for June 19, 1953. On June 17 Justice William O. Douglas granted a last minute stay of execution to consider their seventh appeal.

On June 18 the Supreme Court, meeting in special session, reviewed Justice Douglas' stay. On June 19, 1953 the Court announced their 6-3 *per curiam* decision [by the Court majority without attribution of authorship]. The edited text of the *per curiam* decision, a concurrence by Justice Tom Clark, and a dissent by Justice William O. Douglas follow.

THE ROSENBERG COURT

Chief Justice Frederick M. Vinson
Appointed by President Truman
Served 1946 - 1953

Associate Justice Hugo Black
Appointed by President Franklin Roosevelt
Served 1937 - 1971

Associate Justice Stanley Reed
Appointed by President Franklin Roosevelt
Served 1938 - 1957

Associate Justice Felix Frankfurter
Appointed by President Franklin Roosevelt
Served 1939 - 1962

Associate Justice William O. Douglas
Appointed by President Franklin Roosevelt
Served 1939 - 1975

Associate Justice Robert H. Jackson
Appointed by President Franklin Roosevelt
Served 1941 - 1954

Associate Justice Harold Burton
Appointed by President Truman
Served 1945 - 1958

Associate Justice Tom Clark
Appointed by President Truman
Served 1949 - 1967

Associate Justice Sherman Minton
Appointed by President Truman
Served 1949 - 1956

The unedited text of *Julius and Ethel Rosenberg v. United States* can be found on page 273, volume 346, of *United States Reports*.

JULIUS & ETHEL ROSENBERG
v. UNITED STATES
JUNE 19, 1953

PER CURIAM [by the whole Court]: . . . . The question which has been and now is urged as being substantial is whether the provisions of the Atomic Energy Act of 1946 rendered the District Court powerless to impose the death sentence under the Espionage Act of 1917, under which statute the indictment [charge] was laid.

Although this question was raised and presented for the first time to Justice Douglas by counsel who have never been employed by the Rosenbergs, and who heretofore have not participated in this case, the full Court has considered it. . . .

We think the question is not substantial. We think further proceedings to litigate it are unwarranted. A conspiracy was charged and proved to violate the Espionage Act in wartime. The Atomic Energy Act did not repeal or limit the provisions of the Espionage Act. Accordingly, we vacate [annul] the stay [order stopping an act] entered by Justice Douglas on June 17, 1953. . . .

JUSTICE CLARK [joined by Chief Justice Vinson, and Justices Reed, Jackson, Burton, and Minton]: Seven times now have the defendants [the Rosenbergs] been before this Court. In addition, The Chief Justice, as well as individual Justices, has considered applications by the [Rosenbergs]. The Court of Appeals and the District Court have likewise given careful consideration to even more numerous applications than has this Court.

The [Rosenbergs] were sentenced to death on April 5, 1951. Beginning with our refusal to review the conviction and sentence in October 1952, each of the Justices has given the most painstaking consideration to the case. In fact, all during the past Term of this Court one or another facet of this litigation occupied the attention of the Court. At a Special Term on June 15, 1953, we denied for the sixth time the [Rosenbergs'] plea. The next day an application was presented to Justice Douglas, contending that the penalty provisions of the Atomic Energy Act governed this prosecution; and that, since the jury did not find that the [Rosenbergs] committed the charged acts with intent to injure the United States nor recommend the imposition of the death penalty, the court had no power to impose the sentence of death. After a hearing Justice Douglas . . . granted a stay of execution. The Court convened in Special Term to review that determination.

Human lives are at stake; we need not turn this decision on fine points of procedure or a party's technical standing [right] to claim relief. Nor did Justice Douglas lack the power and, in view of his firm belief that the legal issues tendered him were substantial, he even had the duty to grant a temporary stay. But for me the short answer to the contention that the Atomic Energy Act of 1946 may invalidate [the Rosenbergs'] death sentence is that the Atomic Energy Act cannot here apply. It is true [the] Act authorized capital punishment only upon recommendation of a jury and a finding that the offense was committed with intent to injure the United States. (Notably, by that statute the death penalty may be imposed for *peacetime* offenses as well, thus exceeding in harshness the penalties provided by the Espionage Act.) This prosecution, however, charged a wartime violation of the Espionage Act of 1917 under which these elements are not prerequisite to a sentence of death. Where Congress by more than one statute proscribes [prohibits] a private course of conduct, the Government may choose to invoke either applicable law. . . . Nor can the partial overlap of two statutes work a *pro tanto* [as far as it may go] repealer of the earlier Act. When there are two acts upon the same subject, the rule is to give effect to both if possible. . . . There must be "a positive repugnancy between the provisions of the new law, and those of the old." Otherwise the Government when charging a conspiracy to transmit both atomic and non-atomic secrets would have to split its prosecution into two alleged crimes. [T]he Atomic Energy Act itself, moreover, expressly provides that [it] "shall not exclude the applicable provisions of any other laws . . . ," an unmistakable reference to the 1917 Espionage Act. Therefore this section of the Atomic Energy Act, instead of repealing the penalty provisions of the Espionage Act, in fact preserves them in undiminished force. Thus there is no warrant for superimposing the penalty provisions of the later Act upon the earlier law.

In any event, the Government could not have invoked the Atomic Energy Act against [the Rosenbergs]. The crux of the charge alleged overt acts committed in 1944 and 1945, years before that Act went into effect. While some overt acts did in fact take place as late as 1950, they related principally to [the Rosenbergs'] efforts to avoid detection and prosecution of earlier deeds. . . . Since the Atomic Energy Act . . . cannot cover the offenses charged, the alleged inconsistency of its penalty provisions with those of the Espionage Act cannot be sustained [maintained].

Our liberty is maintained only so long as justice is secure. To permit our judicial processes to be used to obstruct the course of justice destroys our freedom. Over two years ago the Rosenbergs were found guilty by a jury of a grave offense in time of war. Unlike other litigants they have had the attention of this Court seven times; each time their pleas have been denied. Though the penalty is great and our responsibility heavy, our duty is clear.

JUSTICE DOUGLAS, dissenting: When the motion [request to the court] for a stay [order stopping an act] was before me, I was deeply troubled by the legal question tendered. After twelve hours of research and study I concluded, as my opinion indicated, that the question was a substantial one, never presented to this Court and never decided by any court. So I issued the stay order.

Now I have had the benefit of an additional argument and additional study and reflection. Now I know that I am right on the law.

The Solicitor General says in oral argument that the Government would have been laughed out of court if the indictment in this case had been laid under the Atomic Energy Act of 1946. I agree. For a part of the crime alleged [charged] and proved antedated that Act. And obviously no criminal statute can have retroactive application. But the Solicitor General misses the legal point on which my stay order was based. It is this - whether or not the death penalty can be imposed *without the recommendation of the jury* for a crime involving the disclosure of atomic secrets where a part of that crime takes place after the effective date of the Atomic Energy Act.

The crime of the Rosenbergs was a conspiracy that started prior to the Atomic Energy Act and continued almost 4 years after the effective date of that Act. The overt acts *alleged* were acts which took place prior to the effective date of the new Act. But that is irrelevant for two reasons. *First,* acts in pursuance of the conspiracy were proved which took place *after* the new Act became the law. *Second,* under *Singer v. United States,* no overt acts were necessary; the crime was complete when the conspiracy was proved. And that conspiracy, as defined in the indictment [charge] itself, endured almost 4 years after the Atomic Energy Act became effective.

The crime therefore took place in substantial part *after* the new Act became effective, *after* Congress had written new penalties for conspiracies to disclose atomic secrets. One of the new requirements is that the death penalty for that kind of espionage can be imposed *only* if the jury recommends it. And here there was no such recommendation. To be sure, this espionage included more than atomic secrets. But there can be no doubt that the death penalty was imposed because of the Rosenbergs' disclosure of atomic secrets. The trial judge, in sentencing the Rosenbergs to death, emphasized that the heinous character of their crime was trafficking in atomic secrets. He said:

> "I believe your conduct in putting into the hands of the Russians the A-bomb years before our best scientists predicted Russia would perfect the bomb has already caused, in my opinion, the Communist aggression in Korea, with the resultant casualties exceeding 50,000 and who knows but that millions more of innocent people may pay the price of your treason. Indeed, by your betrayal you undoubtedly have altered the course of history to the disadvantage of our country."

But the Congress in 1946 adopted new criminal sanctions
for such crimes. Whether Congress was wise or unwise in
doing so is no question for us. The cold truth is that the
death sentence may not be imposed for what the Rosenbergs did unless the jury so recommends.

Some say, however, that since *a part* of the Rosenbergs'
crime was committed under the old law, the penalties of
the old law apply. But it is law too elemental . . . that
where two penal statutes may apply - one carrying death,
the other imprisonment - the court has no choice but to
impose the less harsh sentence.

A suggestion is made that the question comes too late, that
since the Rosenbergs did not raise this question on appeal,
they are barred from raising it now. But the question of
an unlawful sentence is never barred. No man or woman
should go to death under an unlawful sentence merely because his lawyer failed to raise the point. It is that function among others that the Great Writ [the writ of *habeas
corpus* (an order to bring a person before the court)]
serves. I adhere to the views stated by Chief Justice
Hughes for a unanimous Court in *Bowen v. Johnston.* "It
must never be forgotten that the writ of *habeas corpus* is
the precious safeguard of personal liberty and there is no
higher duty than to maintain it unimpaired. . . ."

Here the trial court was without jurisdiction [authority] to
impose the death penalty, since the jury had not recommended it.

Before the present argument I knew only that the question was serious and substantial. Now I am sure of the an-

swer. I know deep in my heart that I am right on the law. Knowing that, my duty is clear.

Their last appeal denied by the Supreme Court, the Rosenbergs requested a grant of executive clemency from President Dwight D. Eisenhower.

In denying their request, President Eisenhower responded: "I can only say that, by immeasurably increasing the chance of atomic war, the Rosenbergs may have condemned to death tens of millions of innocent people all over the world."

On the night of June 19, 1953, in the Death House at Sing Sing Prison, Julius and Ethel Rosenberg were executed by electrocution.

LIBEL

The New York Times v. Sullivan

As the whole world knows by now, thousands of Southern Negro students are engaged in widespread non-violent demonstrations in positive affirmation of the right to live in human dignity as guaranteed by the U.S. Constitution and the Bill of Rights.

Heed Their Rising Voices

On March 29, 1960 The Committee to Defend Martin Luther King purchased a full-page advertisement in the *New York Times* entitled *Heed Their Rising Voices.*

In paragraphs three and six of *Heed Their Rising Voices,* the Montgomery Alabama Police were charged with the mistreatment of non-violent civil rights protesters and their leader, the Reverend Dr. Martin Luther King, Jr.

The daily circulation of the *New York Times* that day was about 650,000. 394 copies were sent to Alabama and, of those, 35 copies circulated in Montgomery County. One of those copies went to L.B. Sullivan, Montgomery, Alabama Commissioner of Public Affairs. Sullivan, who supervised the Montgomery Police, sued the *New York Times* for libel. Although not mentioned by name, Sullivan charged that paragraphs three and six of *Heed Their Rising Voices* contained falsehoods intended to injure his reputation. The *New York Times* answered that they were protected from charges of libel made by a public official under the First Amendment's guarantee of a free press.

A Montgomery County Circuit Court jury awarded Sullivan $500,000. The Alabama Supreme Court affirmed. The *Times* appealed to the United States Supreme Court.

Oral arguments commenced on January 6, 1964. On March 9, 1964 Justice William Brennan announced the 9-0 decision of the Court. The edited text follows.

THE SULLIVAN COURT

Chief Justice Earl Warren
Appointed by President Eisenhower
Served 1953 - 1969

Associate Justice Hugo Black
Appointed by President Franklin Roosevelt
Served 1937 - 1971

Associate Justice William O. Douglas
Appointed by President Franklin Roosevelt
Served 1939 - 1975

Associate Justice Tom Clark
Appointed by President Truman
Served 1949 - 1967

Associate Justice John Marshall Harlan
Appointed by President Eisenhower
Served 1955 - 1971

Associate Justice William J. Brennan, Jr.
Appointed by President Eisenhower
Served 1956 - 1990

Associate Justice Potter Stewart
Appointed by President Eisenhower
Served 1958 - 1981

Associate Justice Byron White
Appointed by President Kennedy
Served 1962 - 1993

Associate Justice Arthur Goldberg
Appointed by President Kennedy
Served 1962 - 1965

The unedited text of *New York Times v. Sullivan* can be found on page 254, volume 376, of *United States Reports*.

THE NEW YORK TIMES v.
L.B. SULLIVAN
MARCH 9, 1964

JUSTICE BRENNAN: We are required in this case to determine for the first time the extent to which the constitutional protections for speech and press limit a State's power to award damages in a libel action [suit for publication of material injurious to one's reputation] brought by a public official against critics of his official conduct.

Respondent L.B. Sullivan is one of the three elected Commissioners of the City of Montgomery, Alabama. He testified that he was "Commissioner of Public Affairs and the duties are supervision of the Police Department, Fire Department, Department of Cemetery and Department of Scales." He brought this . . . libel action against the four individual petitioners, who are Negroes and Alabama clergymen, and against petitioner the New York Times Company, a New York corporation which publishes the *New York Times*, a daily newspaper. A jury in the Circuit Court of Montgomery County awarded him damages of $500,000, the full amount claimed, against all the petitioners, and the Supreme Court of Alabama affirmed [upheld].

[Sullivan]'s complaint alleged that he had been libeled by statements in a full-page advertisement that was carried in the *New York Times* on March 29, 1960. Entitled "Heed Their Rising Voices." The advertisement began by stating that "As the whole world knows by now, thousands of Southern Negro students are engaged in widespread non-violent demonstrations in positive affirmation of the right to live in human dignity as guaranteed by the U.S. Consti-

tution and the Bill of Rights." It went on to charge that
"in their efforts to uphold these guarantees, they are being
met by an unprecedented wave of terror by those who
would deny and negate that document which the whole
world looks upon as setting the pattern for modern freedom. . . ." Succeeding paragraphs purported
to illustrate the "wave of terror" by describing certain alleged events. The text concluded with an appeal for
funds for three purposes; support of the student movement, "the struggle for the right-to-vote," and the legal defense of Dr. Martin Luther King, Jr., leader of the movement, against a perjury [lying under oath] indictment
[charge] then pending in Montgomery.

The text appeared over the names of 64 persons, many
widely known for their activities in public affairs, religion, trade unions, and the performing arts. Below these
names, and under a line reading "We in the south who are
struggling daily for dignity and freedom warmly endorse
this appeal," appeared the names of the four individual
petitioners and of 16 other persons, all but two of whom
were identified as clergymen in various Southern cities.
The advertisement was signed at the bottom of the page
by the "Committee to Defend Martin Luther King and the
Struggle for Freedom in the South," and the officers of
the Committee were listed.

Of the 10 paragraphs of text in the advertisement, the
third and a portion of the sixth were the basis of
[Sullivan]'s claim of libel. They read as follows:

Third paragraph:

> "In Montgomery, Alabama, after students sang
> 'My Country, 'Tis of Thee' on the State Capitol

steps, their leaders were expelled from school, and truckloads of police armed with shotguns and tear-gas ringed the Alabama State College Campus. When the entire student body protested to state authorities by refusing to re-register, their dining hall was padlocked in an attempt to starve them into submission."

Sixth paragraph:

"Again and again the Southern violators have answered Dr. King's peaceful protests with intimidation and violence. They have bombed his home almost killing his wife and child. They have assaulted his person. They have arrested him seven times - for 'speeding', 'loitering' and similar 'offenses.' And now they have charged him with 'perjury' - a *felony* [a crime of a serious nature] under which they could imprison him for *ten years*...."

Although neither of these statements mentions [Sullivan] by name, he contended that the word "police" in the third paragraph referred to him as the Montgomery Commissioner who supervised the Police Department, so that he was being accused of "ringing" the campus with police. He further claimed that the paragraph would be read as imputing to the police, and hence to him, the padlocking of the dining hall in order to starve the students into submission. As to the sixth paragraph, he contended that since arrests are ordinarily made by the police, the statement "They have arrested [Dr. King] seven times" would be read as referring to him; he further contended that the "They" who did the arresting would be equated with the "They" who committed the other described acts and with the "Southern violators." Thus, he argued, the paragraph would be read as accusing the Montgomery police, and hence him, of answering Dr. King's protests with "intimidation and violence," bombing his home, assaulting his person, and charging him with perjury. [Sullivan] and six other Montgomery residents testified that they read some or all of the statements as referring to him in his capacity as Commissioner.

It is uncontroverted that some of the statements contained in the two paragraphs were not accurate descriptions of events which occurred in Montgomery. Although Negro students staged a demonstration on the State Capitol steps, they sang the National Anthem and not "My Country, 'Tis of Thee." Although nine students were expelled by the State Board of Education, this was not for leading the demonstration at the Capitol, but for demanding service at a lunch counter in the Montgomery County Courthouse on another day. Not the entire student body, but most of it, had protested the expulsion, not by refusing to register, but by boycotting classes on a single day; virtually all the students did register for the ensuing semester. The campus dining hall was not padlocked on any occasion, and the only students who may have been barred from eating there were the few who had neither signed a preregistration application nor requested temporary meal tickets. Although the police were deployed near the campus in large numbers on three occasions, they did not at any time "ring" the campus, and they were not called to the campus in connection with the demonstration on the State Capitol steps, as the third paragraph implied. Dr. King had not been arrested seven times, but only four; and although he claimed to have been assaulted some years earlier in connection with his arrest for loitering outside a courtroom, one of the officers who made the arrest denied that there was such an assault.

On the premise that the charges in the sixth paragraph could be read as referring to him, [Sullivan] was allowed to prove that he had not participated in the events described. Although Dr. King's home had in fact been bombed twice when his wife and child were there, both of these occasions antedated [Sullivan]'s tenure as Commissioner, and the police were not only not implicated in the bombings, but had made every effort to apprehend those who were.

Three of Dr. King's four arrests took place before [Sullivan] became Commissioner. Although Dr. King had in fact been indicted (he was subsequently acquitted [released]) on two counts of perjury, each of which carried a possible five-year sentence, [Sullivan] had nothing to do with procuring the indictment.

[Sullivan] made no effort to prove that he suffered actual pecuniary loss as a result of the alleged libel. One of his witnesses, a former employer, testified that if he had believed the statements, he doubted whether he "would want to be associated with anybody who would be a party to such things that are stated in that ad," and that he would not re-employ [Sullivan] if he believed "that he allowed the Police Department to do the things that the paper say he did." But neither this witness nor any of the others testified that he had actually believed the statements in their supposed reference to [Sullivan].

The cost of the advertisement was approximately $4800, and it was published by the *Times* upon an order from a New York advertising agency acting for the signatory

Committee. The agency submitted the advertisement with a letter from A. Philip Randolph, Chairman of the Committee, certifying that the persons whose names appeared on the advertisement had given their permission. Mr. Randolph was known to the *Times'* Advertising Acceptability Department as a responsible person, and in accepting the letter as sufficient proof of authorization it followed its established practice. There was testimony that the copy of the advertisement which accompanied the letter listed only the 64 names appearing under the text, and that the statement, "We in the south . . . warmly endorse this appeal," and the list of names thereunder, which included those of the individual petitioners, were subsequently added when the first proof of the advertisement was received. Each of the individual petitioners testified that he had not authorized the use of his name, and that he had been unaware of its use until receipt of [Sullivan]'s demand for a retraction. The manager of the Advertising Acceptability Department testified that he had approved the advertisement for publication because he knew nothing to cause him to believe that anything in it was false, and because it bore the endorsement of "a number of people who are well known and whose reputation" he "had no reason to question." Neither he nor anyone else at the *Times* made an effort to confirm the accuracy of the advertisement, either by checking it against recent *Times* news stories relating to some of the described events or by any other means.

Alabama law denies a public officer recovery of punitive damages in a libel action brought on account of a publication concerning his official conduct unless he first makes a written demand for a public retraction and the defendant [accused person] fails or refuses to comply. [Sullivan] served such a demand upon each of the petitioners. None of the individual petitioners responded to the demand, primarily because each took the position that he had not authorized the use of his name on the advertisement and therefore had not published the statements that [Sullivan] alleged had libeled him. The *Times* did not publish a retraction in response to the demand, but wrote [Sullivan] a letter stating, among other things, that "we . . . are somewhat puzzled as to how you think the statements in any way reflect on you," and "you might, if you desire, let us know in what respect you claim that the statements in the advertisement reflect on you." Sullivan filed this suit a few days later without answering the letter. The *Times* did, however, subsequently publish a retraction of the advertisement upon the demand of Governor John Patterson of Alabama, who asserted that the publication charged him with "grave misconduct and . . . improper actions and omissions as Governor of Alabama and Ex-Officio Chairman of the State Board of Education of Alabama." When asked to explain why there had been a retraction for the Governor but not for [Sullivan], the Secretary of the *Times* testified: "We did that because we didn't want anything that was published by the *Times* to be a reflection on the State of Alabama and the Governor was, as far as we could see, the embodiment of the State of Alabama and the proper representative of the State and, furthermore, we had by that time learned more of the actual facts which the ad purported to recite and, finally, the ad did refer to the action of the State authorities and the Board of Education presumably of which the Governor is the ex-officio chairman. . . ." On the other hand, he testified that he did not think that "any of the language in there referred to Mr. Sullivan."

. . . . In affirming the judgment, the Supreme Court of Alabama sustained [maintained] the trial judge's rulings

and . . . held that "where the words published tend to injure a person libeled by them in his reputation, profession,
trade or business, or charge him with an indictable offense, or tend to bring the individual into public contempt," they are "libelous per se"; that "the matter complained of is, under the above doctrine, libelous per se, if
it was published of and concerning the plaintiff"; and that
it was actionable without "proof of pecuniary injury . . . ,
such injury being implied." It approved the trial court's
ruling that the jury could find the statements to have
been made "of and concerning" [Sullivan], stating: "We
think it common knowledge that the average person
knows that municipal agents, such as police and firemen,
and others, are under the control and direction of the city
governing body, and more particularly under the direction
and control of a single commissioner. In measuring the
performance or deficiencies of such groups, praise or criticism is usually attached to the official in complete control of the body." In sustaining the trial court's determination that the verdict was not excessive, the court said
that malice could be inferred from the *Times'*
"irresponsibility" in printing the advertisement while "the
Times in its own files had articles already published
which would have demonstrated the falsity of the allegations in the advertisement"; from the *Times'* failure to re-
tract for [Sullivan] while retracting for the Governor,
whereas the falsity of some of the allegations was then
known to the *Times* and "the matter contained in the advertisement was equally false as to both parties"; and
from the testimony of the *Times'* Secretary that, apart
from the statement that the dining hall was padlocked, he
thought the two paragraphs were "substantially correct."
The court reaffirmed a statement in an earlier opinion
that "There is no legal measure of damages in cases of this
character." It rejected petitioners' constitutional conten-

tions with the brief statements that "The First Amendment of the U.S. Constitution does not protect libelous publications" and "The Fourteenth Amendment is directed against State action and not private action."

Because of the importance of the constitutional issues involved, we granted the separate petitions for certiorari [asking a higher court to hear the case] of the individual petitioners and of the *Times.* We reverse the judgment. We hold that the rule of law applied by the Alabama courts is constitutionally deficient for failure to provide the safeguards for freedom of speech and of the press that are required by the First and Fourteenth Amendments in a libel action brought by a public official against critics of his official conduct. We further hold that under the proper safeguards the evidence presented in this case is constitutionally insufficient to support the judgment for [Sullivan].

The Court in *Chrestensen* reaffirmed the constitutional protection for "the freedom of communicating information and disseminating opinion." . . .

The publication here . . . communicated information, expressed opinion, recited grievances, protested claimed abuses, and sought financial support on behalf of a movement whose existence and objectives are matters of the highest public interest and concern. That the *Times* was paid for publishing the advertisement is as immaterial in this connection as is the fact that newspapers and books are sold. Any other conclusion would discourage newspapers from carrying "editorial advertisements" of this type, and so might shut off an important outlet for the promulgation of information and ideas by persons who do not themselves have access to publishing facilities - who wish to exercise their freedom of speech even though they are not members of the press. The effect would be to shackle the First Amendment in its attempt to secure "the widest possible dissemination of information from diverse and antagonistic sources." To avoid placing such a handicap upon the freedoms of expression, we hold that if the allegedly libelous statements would otherwise be constitutionally protected from the present judgment, they do not forfeit that protection because they were published in the form of a paid advertisement.

Under Alabama law as applied in this case, a publication is "libelous per se" if words "tend to injure a person . . . in his reputation" or to "bring [him] into public contempt"; the trial court stated that the standard was met if the words are such as to "injure him in his public office, or impute misconduct to him in his office, or want of official integrity, or want of fidelity to a public trust . . . ." The jury must find that the words were published "of and concerning" the plaintiff [a person who brings a case to the court], but where the plaintiff is a public official his place in the governmental hierarchy is sufficient evidence to support a finding that his reputation has been affected by statements that reflect upon the agency of which he is in charge. Once "libel per se" has been established, the defendant has no defense as to stated facts unless he can persuade the jury that they were true in all their particulars. His privilege of "fair comment" for expressions of opinion depends on the truth of the facts upon which the comment is based. . . .

The question before us is whether this rule of liability, as applied to an action brought by a public official against critics of his official conduct, abridges the freedom of

speech and of the press that is guaranteed by the First and
Fourteenth Amendments.

In *Beauharnais v. Illinois*, the Court sustained an Illinois
criminal libel statute as applied to a publication held to be
both defamatory of a racial group and "liable to cause violence and disorder." But the Court was careful to note
that it "retains and exercises authority to nullify action
which encroaches on freedom of utterance under the
guise of punishing libel"; for "public men, are, as it were,
public property," and "discussion cannot be denied and the
right, as well as the duty, of criticism must not be stifled."
In the only previous case that did present the question of
constitutional limitations upon the power to award damages for libel of a public official (*Schenectady Union Pub.
Co. v. Sweeney*), the Court was equally divided and the
question was not decided. In deciding the question now,
we are compelled by neither precedent [an earlier case
which establishes the rule to be followed] nor policy to
give any more weight to the epithet "libel" than we have
to other "mere labels" of state law. Like insurrection, contempt, advocacy of unlawful acts, breach of the peace, obscenity, solicitation of legal business, and the various other
formulae for the repression of expression that have been
challenged in this Court, libel can claim no talismanic immunity from constitutional limitations. It must be meas-
ured by standards that satisfy the First Amendment.

The general proposition that freedom of expression upon
public questions is secured by the First Amendment has
long been settled by our decisions. The constitutional
safeguard, we have said, "was fashioned to assure unfet-
tered interchange of ideas for the bringing about of political and social changes desired by the people. The maintenance of the opportunity for free political discussion to

the end that government may be responsive to the will of
the people and that changes may be obtained by lawful
means, an opportunity essential to the security of the Re-
public, is a fundamental principle of our constitutional
system." "[I]t is a prized American privilege to speak
one's mind, although not always with perfect good taste,
on all public institutions," and this opportunity is to be afforded for "vigorous advocacy" no less than "abstract discussion." The First Amendment, said Judge Learned
Hand, "presupposes that right conclusions are more likely
to be gathered out of a multitude of tongues, than through
any kind of authoritative selection. To many this is, and
always will be, folly; but we have staked upon it our all."
Justice Brandeis, in his concurring opinion in *Whitney v.
California*, gave the principle its classic formulation:

"Those who won our independence believed . . . that public discussion is a political duty; and that this should be a
fundamental principle of the American government.
They recognized the risks to which all human institutions
are subject. But they knew that order cannot be secured
merely through fear of punishment for its infraction; that
it is hazardous to discourage thought, hope and imagination; that fear breeds repression; that repression breeds
hate; that hate menaces stable government; that the path
of safety lies in the opportunity to discuss freely supposed
grievances and proposed remedies; and that the fitting
remedy for evil counsels is good ones. Believing in the
power of reason as applied through public discussion, they
eschewed silence coerced by law the argument of force in
its worst form. Recognizing the occasional tyrannies of
governing majorities, they amended the Constitution so
that free speech and assembly should be guaranteed."

Thus we consider this case against the background of a profound national commitment to the principle that debate on public issues should be uninhibited, robust, and wide-open, and that it may well include vehement, caustic, and sometimes unpleasantly sharp attacks on government and public officials. The present advertisement, as an expression of grievance and protest on one of the major public issues of our time, would seem clearly to qualify for the constitutional protection. The question is whether it forfeits that protection by the falsity of some of its factual statements and by its alleged defamation of [Sullivan].

Authoritative interpretations of the First Amendment guarantees have consistently refused to recognize an exception for any test of truth - whether administered by judges, juries, or administrative officials - and especially one that puts the burden of proving truth on the speaker. The constitutional protection does not turn upon "the truth, popularity, or social utility of the ideas and beliefs which are offered." As Madison said, "Some degree of abuse is inseparable from the proper use of every thing; and in no instance is this more true than in that of the press." In *Cantwell v. Connecticut*, the Court declared:

> "In the realm of religious faith, and in that of political belief, sharp differences arise. In both fields the tenets of one man may seem the rankest error to his neighbor. To persuade others to his own point of view, the pleader, as we know, at times, resorts to exaggeration, to vilification of men who have been, or are, prominent in church or state, and even to false statement. But the people of this nation have ordained in the light of history, that, in spite of the probability of excess-

es and abuses, these liberties are, in the long view,
essential to enlightened opinion and right conduct
on the part of the citizens of a democracy."

. . . . Injury to official reputation affords no more warrant for repressing speech that would otherwise be free
than does factual error. . . .

If neither factual error nor defamatory content suffices to
remove the constitutional shield from criticism of official
conduct, the combination of the two elements is no less inadequate. This is the lesson to be drawn from the great
controversy over the Sedition Act of 1798, which first
crystallized a national awareness of the central meaning
of the First Amendment. That statute made it a crime,
punishable by a $5,000 fine and five years in prison, "if
any person shall write, print, utter or publish . . . any
false, scandalous and malicious writing or writings against
the government of the United States, or either house of
the Congress . . . , or the President . . . , with intent to de-
fame . . . or to bring them, or either of them, into contempt or disrepute; or to excite against them, or either or
any of them, the hatred of the good people of the United
States." The Act allowed the defendant the defense of
truth, and provided that the jury were to be judges both
of the law and the facts. Despite these qualifications, the
Act was vigorously condemned as unconstitutional in an
attack joined in by Jefferson and Madison. In the famous
Virginia Resolutions of 1798, the General Assembly of
Virginia resolved that it "doth particularly protest against
the palpable and alarming infractions of the Constitution,
in the two late cases of the 'Alien and Sedition Acts,'
passed at the last session of Congress. . . . [The Sedition
Act] exercises . . . a power not delegated by the Constitution, but, on the contrary, expressly and positively forbid-

den by one of the amendments thereto - a power which, more than any other, ought to produce universal alarm, because it is levelled against the right of freely examining public characters and measures, and of free communication among the people thereon, which has ever been justly deemed the only effectual guardian of every other right."

Madison prepared the Report in support of the protest. His premise was that the Constitution created a form of government under which "The people, not the government, possess the absolute sovereignty." . . . The right of free public discussion of the stewardship of public officials was thus, in Madison's view, a fundamental principle of the American form of government.

Although the Sedition Act was never tested in this Court, the attack upon its validity has carried the day in the court of history. Fines levied in its prosecution were repaid by Act of Congress on the ground that it was unconstitutional. Jefferson, as President, pardoned those who had been convicted and sentenced under the Act and remitted their fines, stating: "I discharged every person under punishment or prosecution under the sedition law, because I considered, and now consider, that law to be a nullity [void], as absolute and as palpable as if Congress had ordered us to fall down and worship a golden image." The invalidity of the Act has also been assumed by Justices of this Court. These views reflect a broad consensus that the Act, because of the restraint it imposed upon criticism of government and public officials, was inconsistent with the First Amendment.

. . . . It is true that the First Amendment was originally addressed only to action by the Federal Government, and that Jefferson, for one, while denying the power of Con-

gress "to control the freedom of the press," recognized
such a power in the States. But this distinction was eliminated with the adoption of the Fourteenth Amendment
and the application to the States of the First
Amendment's restrictions.

What a State may not constitutionally bring about by
means of a criminal statute is likewise beyond the reach
of its civil law of libel. The fear of damage awards under
a rule such as that invoked by the Alabama courts here
may be markedly more inhibiting than the fear of prosecution under a criminal statute. Alabama, for example,
has a criminal libel law which subjects to prosecution "any
person who speaks, writes, or prints of and concerning
another any accusation falsely and maliciously importing
the commission by such person of a felony, or any other
indictable offense involving moral turpitude," and which
allows as punishment upon conviction a fine not exceeding $500 and a prison sentence of six months. Presuma-
bly a person charged with violation of this statute enjoys
ordinary criminal law safeguards such as the requirements
of an indictment and of proof beyond a reasonable doubt.
These safeguards are not available to the defendant in a
civil action. The judgment awarded in this case - without
the need for any proof of actual pecuniary loss - was one
thousand times greater than the maximum fine provided
by the Alabama criminal statute, and one hundred times
greater than that provided by the Sedition Act. And since
there is no double-jeopardy limitation applicable to civil
lawsuits, this is not the only judgment that may be awarded against petitioners for the same publication. Whether
or not a newspaper can survive a succession of such judgments, the pall of fear and timidity imposed upon those
who would give voice to public criticism is an atmosphere
in which the First Amendment freedoms cannot survive.

Plainly the Alabama law of civil libel is "a form of regulation that creates hazards to protected freedoms markedly greater than those that attend reliance upon the criminal law."

.... Allowance of the defense of truth, with the burden of proving it on the defendant, does not mean that only false speech will be deterred. Even courts accepting this defense as an adequate safeguard have recognized the difficulties of adducing [presenting] legal proofs that the alleged libel was true in all its factual particulars. Under such a rule, would-be critics of official conduct may be deterred from voicing their criticism, even though it is believed to be true and even though it is in fact true, because of doubt whether it can be proved in court or fear of the expense of having to do so. They tend to make only statements which "steer far wider of the unlawful zone." The rule thus dampens the vigor and limits the variety of public debate. It is inconsistent with the First and Fourteenth Amendments.

The constitutional guarantees require, we think, a federal rule that prohibits a public official from recovering damages for a defamatory falsehood relating to his official conduct unless he proves that the statement was made with "actual malice" - that is, with knowledge that it was false or with reckless disregard of whether it was false or not. . . .

We hold today that the Constitution delimits a State's power to award damages for libel in actions brought by public officials against critics of their official conduct. Since this is such an action, the rule requiring proof of actual malice is applicable.

While Alabama law apparently requires proof of actual
malice for an award of punitive damages, where general
damages are concerned malice is "presumed." Such a presumption is inconsistent with the federal rule. "The power to create presumptions is not a means of escape from
constitutional restrictions. The showing of malice required for the forfeiture of the privilege is not presumed
but is a matter for proof by the plaintiff. . . ." Since the
trial judge did not instruct the jury to differentiate between general and punitive damages, it may be that the
verdict was wholly an award of one or the other. But it is
impossible to know, in view of the general verdict returned. Because of this uncertainty, the judgment must be
reversed and the case remanded [sent back to the lower
court].

Since [Sullivan] may seek a new trial, we deem that considerations of effective judicial administration require us
to review the evidence in the present record to determine
whether it could constitutionally support a judgment for
[him]. This Court's duty is not limited to the elaboration
of constitutional principles; we must also in proper cases
review the evidence to make certain that those principles
have been constitutionally applied. This is such a case,
particularly since the question is one of alleged trespass
across "the line between speech unconditionally guaranteed and speech which may legitimately be regulated." In
cases where that line must be drawn, the rule is that we
"examine for ourselves the statements in issue and the circumstances under which they were made to see . . . whether they are of a character which the principles of the First
Amendment, as adopted by the Due Process Clause of the
Fourteenth Amendment, protect." We must "make an independent examination of the whole record," so as to as-

sure ourselves that the judgment does not constitute a forbidden intrusion on the field of free expression.

Applying these standards, we consider that the proof presented to show actual malice lacks the convincing clarity
which the constitutional standard demands, and hence that
it would not constitutionally sustain the judgment for
[Sullivan]. . . . The case of the individual petitioners requires little discussion. Even assuming that they could
constitutionally be found to have authorized the use of
their names on the advertisement, there was no evidence
whatever that they were aware of any erroneous statements or were in any way reckless in that regard. The
judgment against them is thus without constitutional support.

As to the *Times*, we similarly conclude that the facts do
not support a finding of actual malice. The statement by
the *Times'* Secretary that, apart from the padlocking allegation, he thought the advertisement was "substantially
correct," . . . affords no constitutional warrant for the Alabama Supreme Court's conclusion that it was a "cavalier
ignoring of the falsity of the advertisement [from which]
the jury could not have but been impressed with the bad
faith of the *Times*, and its maliciousness inferable therefrom." The statement does not indicate malice at the time
of the publication; even if the advertisement was not
"substantially correct" that opinion was at least a reasonable one, and there was no evidence to impeach the witness' good faith in holding it. The *Times'* failure to re-
tract upon [Sullivan]'s demand, although it later retracted
upon the demand of Governor Patterson, is likewise not
adequate evidence of malice for constitutional purposes.
. . .

Finally, there is evidence that the *Times* published the advertisement without checking its accuracy against the news stories in the *Times'* own files. The mere presence of the stories in the files does not, of course, establish that the *Times* "knew" the advertisement was false, since the state of mind required for actual malice would have to be brought home to the persons in the *Times'* organization having responsibility for the publication of the advertisement. With respect to the failure of those persons to make the check, the record shows that they relied upon their knowledge of the good reputation of many of those whose names were listed as sponsors of the advertisement, and upon the letter from A. Philip Randolph, known to them as a responsible individual, certifying that the use of the names was authorized. There was testimony that the persons handling the advertisement saw nothing in it that would render it unacceptable under the *Times'* policy of rejecting advertisements containing "attacks of a personal character"; their failure to reject it on this ground was not unreasonable. We think the evidence against the *Times* supports at most a finding of negligence in failing to discover the misstatements, and is constitutionally insufficient to show the recklessness that is required for a finding of actual malice.

. . . . There was no reference to [Sullivan] in the advertisement, either by name or official position. A number of the allegedly libelous statements - the charges that the dining hall was padlocked and that Dr. King's home was bombed, his person assaulted, and a perjury prosecution instituted against him - did not even concern the police; despite the ingenuity of the arguments which would attach this significance to the word "They," it is plain that these statements could not reasonably be read as accusing

[Sullivan] of personal involvement in the acts in question. . . .

The judgment of the Supreme Court of Alabama is reversed and the case is remanded to that court for further proceedings not inconsistent with this opinion.

CONSCIENTIOUS OBJECTION

Muhammad Ali v. United States

I am a member of the Muslims and we don't go to war unless they are declared by Allah himself. I don't have no personal quarrel with those Vietcongs.

Muhammad Ali in an interview with the Chicago Daily News, February 18, 1966

On April 18, 1960 Cassius Marsellus Clay, Jr., an 18-year-old amateur boxer, registered, as required by law, with his local Louisville, Kentucky draft board. In 1964, the year he became the heavyweight champion of the world, Cassius Clay joined the Nation of Islam, the Black Muslims, and took the name Muhammad Ali.

On February 17, 1966, during the Viet Nam War buildup, Ali was classified I-A: Available for Military Service. Based on the teaching of his Muslim faith, Ali filed for Conscientious Objector classification: Exempt from Military Service. A conscientious objector must pass each of three tests: 1) he must be be opposed to war in any form, 2) his claim must be based on religious training and belief, and 3) his opposition to war must be sincere.

The Selective Service System, told by the U.S. Department of Justice that Ali had failed to pass the conscientious objector tests, ordered him to report for military induction. On April 28, 1967 Ali refused. Tried and convicted of draft evasion, Ali was sentenced, on June 20, 1967, to five years' imprisonment. In May 1968 the U.S. Court of Appeals upheld his conviction and Muhammad Ali appealed to the United States Supreme Court.

Oral arguments commenced April 19, 1971. On June 28, 1971 the Court announced a 6-2 (Justice Marshall not taking part) *per curiam* decision (by a majority of the Court without attribution of authorship). The edited text follows.

THE ALI COURT

Chief Justice Warren Burger
Appointed by President Nixon
Served 1969 - 1986

Associate Justice Hugo Black
Appointed by President Franklin Roosevelt
Served 1937 - 1971

Associate Justice William O. Douglas
Appointed by President Franklin Roosevelt
Served 1939 - 1975

Associate Justice John Marshall Harlan
Appointed by President Eisenhower
Served 1955 - 1971

Associate Justice William J. Brennan, Jr.
Appointed by President Eisenhower
Served 1956 - 1990

Associate Justice Potter Stewart
Appointed by President Eisenhower
Served 1958 - 1981

Associate Justice Byron White
Appointed by President Kennedy
Served 1962 - 1993

Associate Justice Thurgood Marshall
Appointed by President Lyndon Johnson
Served 1967 - 1991

Associate Justice Harry Blackmun
Appointed by President Nixon
Served 1970 -

The unedited text of *Muhammud Ali v. United States* can
be found on page 698, volume 403, *United States Reports.*

MUHAMMAD ALI v. UNITED STATES
JUNE 28, 1971

PER CURIAM [by the whole Court]: The petitioner [Muhammad Ali] was convicted for willful refusal to submit to induction into the Armed Forces. The judgment of conviction was affirmed [upheld] by the Court of Appeals for the Fifth Circuit. We granted certiorari [agreed to hear the case], to consider whether the induction notice was invalid because grounded upon an erroneous denial of [Ali]'s claim to be classified as a conscientious objector.

[Ali]'s application for classification as a conscientious objector was turned down by his local draft board, and he took an administrative appeal. The State Appeal Board tentatively classified him I-A (eligible for unrestricted military service) and referred his file to the Department of Justice for an advisory recommendation, in accordance with then-applicable procedures. The FBI then conducted an "inquiry" as required by the statute, interviewing some 35 persons, including members of [Ali]'s family and many of his friends, neighbors, and business and religious associates.

There followed a hearing on "the character and good faith of [Ali]'s objections" before a hearing officer appointed by the Department. The hearing officer, a retired judge of many years' experience, heard testimony from [Ali]'s mother and father, from one of his attorneys, from a minister of his religion, and from [Ali] himself. He also had the benefit of a full report from the FBI. On the basis of this record the hearing officer concluded that [Ali] was sincere in his objection on religious grounds to participation in war in any form, and he recommended that the conscientious objector claim be sustained [maintained].

Notwithstanding this recommendation, the Department of Justice wrote a letter to the Appeal Board, advising it that [Ali]'s conscientious objector claim should be denied. Upon receipt of this letter of advice, the Board denied [Ali]'s claim without a statement of reasons. After various further proceedings which it is not necessary to recount here, [Ali] was ordered to report for induction. He refused to take the traditional step forward, and this prosecution and conviction followed.

In order to qualify for classification as a conscientious objector, a registrant must satisfy three basic tests. He must show that he is conscientiously opposed to war in any form. He must show that this opposition is based upon religious training and belief, as the term has been construed [interpreted] in our decisions. And he must show that this objection is sincere. In applying these tests, the Selective Service System must be concerned with the registrant as an individual, not with its own interpretation of the dogma of the religious sect, if any, to which he may belong.

. . . . [Ali]'s criminal conviction stemmed from the Selective Service System's denial of his appeal seeking conscientious objector status. That denial, for which no reasons were ever given, was, as we have said, based on a recommendation of the Department of Justice, overruling its hearing officer and advising the Appeal Board that it "finds that the registrant's conscientious objector claim is not sustained and recommends to your Board that he be not [so] classified." This finding was contained in a long letter of explanation, from which it is evident that Selective Service officials were led to believe that the Department had found that [Ali] had failed to satisfy each of the three basic tests for qualification as a conscientious objector.

As to the requirement that a registrant must be opposed to war in any form, the Department letter said that [Ali]'s expressed beliefs "do not appear to preclude military service in any form, but rather are limited to military service in the Armed Forces of the United States. . . . These constitute only objections to certain types of war in certain circumstances, rather than a general scruple against participation in war in any form. However, only a general scruple against participation in war in any form can support an exemption as a conscientious objector under the Act."

As to the requirement that a registrant's opposition must be based upon religious training and belief, the Department letter said: "It seems clear that the teachings of the Nation of Islam preclude fighting for the United States not because of objections to participation in war in any form but rather because of political and racial objections to policies of the United States as interpreted by Elijah Muhammad. . . . It is therefore our conclusion that registrant's claimed objections to participation in war insofar as they are based upon the teachings of the Nation of Islam, rest on grounds which primarily are political and racial."

As to the requirement that a registrant's opposition to war must be sincere, that part of the letter began by stating that "the registrant has not consistently manifested his conscientious objector claim. Such a course of overt manifestations is requisite to establishing a subjective state of mind and belief." There followed several paragraphs reciting the timing and circumstances of [Ali]'s conscientious objector claim, and a concluding paragraph seeming to state a rule of law - that "a registrant has not shown overt manifestations sufficient to establish his subjective belief where, as here, his conscientious objector claim was not asserted until military service became imminent.

In this Court the Government has now fully conceded that [Ali]'s beliefs *are* based upon "religious training and belief," as defined in *United States v. Seeger.* "There is no dispute that petitioner's [the person presenting the case to the court] professed beliefs were founded on basic tenets of the Muslim religion as he understood them, and derived in substantial part from his devotion to Allah as the Supreme Being. Thus, under this Court's decision in *United States v. Seeger,* his claim unquestionably was within the 'religious training and belief' clause of the exemption provision." This concession is clearly correct. For the record shows that [Ali]'s beliefs are founded on tenets of the Muslim religion as he understands them. They are surely no less religiously based than those of the three registrants before this Court in *Seeger.*

The Government in this Court has also made clear that it no longer questions the sincerity of [Ali]'s beliefs. This concession is also correct. The Department hearing officer - the only person at the administrative appeal level who carefully examined [Ali] and other witnesses in person and who had the benefit of the full FBI file - found "that the registrant is sincere in his objection." The Department of Justice was wrong in advising the Board in terms of a purported rule of law that it should disregard this finding simply because of the circumstances and timing of [Ali]'s claim.

Since the Appeal Board gave no reasons for its denial of [Ali]'s claim, there is absolutely no way of knowing upon which of the three grounds offered in the Department's letter it relied. Yet the Government now acknowledges that two of those grounds were not valid. And, the Government's concession aside, it is indisputably clear, for the reasons stated, that the Department was simply wrong as a matter of law in advising that [Ali]'s beliefs were not religiously based and were not sincerely held.

This case, therefore, falls squarely within the four corners of this Court's decision in *Sicurella v. United States.* There as here the Court was asked to hold that an error in an advice letter prepared by the Department of Justice did not require reversal of a criminal conviction because there was a ground on which the Appeal Board might properly have denied a conscientious objector classification. This Court refused to consider the proferred alternative ground:

> "[W]e feel that this error of law by the Department, to which the Appeal Board might naturally look for guidance on such questions, must vitiate the entire proceedings at least not where it is not clear that the Board relied on some legitimate ground. Here, where it is impossible to determine on exactly which grounds the Appeal Board decided, the integrity of the Selective Service System demands, at least, that the Government not recommend illegal grounds. There is an impressive body of lower court cases taking this position and we believe that they state the correct rule."

The doctrine thus articulated 16 years ago in *Sicurella* was hardly new. It was long ago established as essential to the administration of criminal justice. In *Stromberg* the Court reversed a conviction for violation of a California statute containing three separate clauses, finding one of the three clauses constitutionally invalid. As Chief Justice Hughes put the matter, "[I]t is impossible to say under which clause of the statute the conviction was obtained." Thus, "if any of the clauses in question is invalid under the Federal Constitution, the conviction cannot be upheld."

The application of this doctrine in the area of Selective Service law goes back at least to 1945, and Judge Learned Hand's opinion for the Second Circuit in *United States v. Cain*. It is a doctrine that has been consistently and repeatedly followed by the federal courts in dealing with the criminal sanctions of the selective service laws. In every one of the above cases the defendant was acquitted [set free] or the conviction set aside under the *Sicurella* application of the *Stromberg* doctrine.

The long established rule of law embodied in these settled precedents [earlier cases that define the law] thus clearly requires that the judgment before us be reversed.

On April 30, 1967, two days after his refusal to be inducted, the World Boxing Association stripped Muhammad Ali of the heavyweight championship he had held since 1964.

On October 30, 1974 Muhammad Ali regained the heavyweight championship of the world, defeating George Forman. Ali retired from boxing in 1979.

HATE CRIMES

R.A.V. v. St. Paul

Whoever places on public or private property a symbol, object, appellation, characterization or graffiti, including, but not limited to, a burning cross or Nazi swastika, which one knows or has reasonable grounds to know arouses anger, alarm or resentment in others on the basis of race, creed, religion, or gender commits disorderly conduct and shall be guilty of a misdemeanor.

Hate Crime Ordinance
City of St. Paul, Minnesota

On June 21, 1990, a teenager identified in court records only as R.A.V., allegedly participated with other teenagers in a cross burning on the property of a black family in the City of St. Paul, Minnesota. R.A.V. was charged as a juvenile with a violation of the 1990 City of St. Paul Hate Crime Ordinance, which prohibited the display of the symbols of hate - including the burning cross. The trial court dismissed this charge against R.A.V. on the grounds that the wording of St. Paul's Hate Crime Ordinance was both (1) overbroad - the phrase "arouse anger, alarm, or resentment in others" was too non-specific, and (2) impermissibly content-based - the St. Paul Hate Crime Ordinance imposed special, therefore impermissible, restrictions on a person's freedom to speak on the subjects of race, creed, religion or gender, a violation of the First Amendment. The City of St. Paul appealed to the Minnesota Supreme Court, which reversed this decision. R.A.V. appealed to the United States Supreme Court.

Oral arguments commenced December 4, 1991. On June 22, 1992 Justice Antonin Scalia announced the 9-0 decision of the Court. The edited text follows.

THE R.A.V. COURT

Chief Justice William Rehnquist
Appointed Chief Justice by President Reagan
Appointed Associate Justice by President Nixon
Served 1971 -

Associate Justice Byron White
Appointed by President Kennedy
Served 1962 - 1993

Associate Justice Harry Blackmun
Appointed by President Nixon
Served 1970 -

Associate Justice John Paul Stevens
Appointed by President Ford
Served 1975 -

Associate Justice Sandra Day O'Connor
Appointed by President Reagan
Served 1981 -

Associate Justice Antonin Scalia
Appointed by President Reagan
Served 1976 -

Associate Justice Anthony Kennedy
Appointed by President Reagan
Served 1988 -

Associate Justice David Souter
Appointed by President Bush
Served 1991 -

Associate Justice Clarence Thomas
Appointed by President Bush
Served 1991 -

The full text of *R.A. V. v. St. Paul* can be found in volume 505 of *United States Reports.*

R.A.V. v. ST. PAUL
JUNE 22, 1992

JUSTICE SCALIA: In the predawn hours of June 21, 1990, petitioner [R.A.V.] and several other teenagers allegedly assembled a crudely-made cross by taping together broken chair legs. They then allegedly burned the cross inside the fenced yard of a black family that lived across the street from the house where [R.A.V.] was staying. Although this conduct could have been punished under any of a number of laws, one of the two provisions under which respondent city of St. Paul chose to charge [R.A.V.] (then a juvenile) was the St. Paul Bias-Motivated Crime Ordinance, which provides:

> "Whoever places on public or private property a symbol, object, appellation, characterization or graffiti, including, but not limited to, a burning cross or Nazi swastika, which one knows or has reasonable grounds to know arouses anger, alarm or resentment in others on the basis of race, color, creed, religion or gender commits disorderly conduct and shall be guilty of a misdemeanor."

[R.A.V.] moved to dismiss this count [charge]. . . . The trial court granted this motion but the Minnesota Supreme Court reversed. . . . The court also concluded that . . . "the ordinance is a narrowly tailored means toward accomplishing the compelling governmental interest in protecting the community against bias-motivated threats to public safety and order." We granted certiorari [agreed to hear the case].

In construing [interpreting] the St. Paul ordinance, we are bound by the construction given to it by the Minnesota

court. Accordingly, we accept the Minnesota Supreme
Court's authoritative statement that the ordinance reaches
only those expressions that constitute "fighting words"
within the meaning of *Chaplinsky*. . . . Assuming, [for the
sake of argument,] that all of the expression reached by
the ordinance is proscribable [forbidden] under the
"fighting words" doctrine, we nonetheless conclude that
the ordinance is facially unconstitutional in that it prohibits otherwise permitted speech solely on the basis of the
subjects the speech addresses.

The First Amendment generally prevents government
from proscribing speech, or even expressive conduct, because of disapproval of the ideas expressed. . . . From
1791 to the present, however, our society, like other free
but civilized societies, has permitted restrictions upon the
content of speech in a few limited areas, which are "of
such slight social value as a step to truth that any benefit
that may be derived from them is clearly outweighed by
the social interest in order and morality." We have recognized that "the freedom of speech" referred to by the
First Amendment does not include a freedom to disregard
these traditional limitations. Our decisions since the
1960's have narrowed the scope of the traditional categorical exceptions for defamation, and for obscenity, but a
limited categorical approach has remained an important
part of our First Amendment jurisprudence [science of
law].

We have sometimes said that these categories of expression are "not within the area of constitutionally protected
speech," or that the "protection of the First Amendment
does not extend" to them. Such statements must be taken
in context, however, and are no more literally true than is
the occasionally repeated shorthand characterizing obscen-

ity "as not being speech at all." What they mean is that these areas of speech can, consistently with the First Amendment, be regulated *because of their constitutionally proscribable content* (obscenity, defamation, etc.) - not that they are categories of speech entirely invisible to the Constitution, so that they may be made the vehicles for content discrimination unrelated to their distinctively proscribable content. Thus, the government may proscribe libel [the publication of something harmful to one's reputation]; but it may not make the further content discrimination of proscribing *only* libel critical of the government. We recently acknowledged this distinction in *Ferber*, where, in upholding New York's child pornography law, we expressly recognized that there was no "question here of censoring a particular literary theme. . . ."

Our cases surely do not establish the proposition that the First Amendment imposes no obstacle whatsoever to regulation of particular instances of such proscribable expression, so that the government "may regulate [them] freely." That would mean that a city council could enact an ordinance prohibiting only those legally obscene works that contain criticism of the city government or, indeed, that do not include endorsement of the city government. Such a simplistic, all-or-nothing-at-all approach to First Amendment protection is at odds with common sense and with our jurisprudence [science of law] as well. It is not true that "fighting words" have at most a "de minimis" [an insignificant] expressive content, or that their content is *in all respects* "worthless and undeserving of constitutional protection"; sometimes they are quite expressive indeed. We have not said that they constitute "*no* part of the expression of ideas," but only that they constitute "no *essential* part of any exposition of ideas."

The proposition that a particular instance of speech can be proscribable on the basis of one feature (e.g., obscenity) but not on the basis of another (e.g., opposition to the city government) is commonplace, and has found application in many contexts. We have long held, for example, that nonverbal expressive activity can be banned because of the action it entails, but not because of the ideas it expresses - so that burning a flag in violation of an ordinance against outdoor fires could be punishable, whereas burning a flag in violation of an ordinance against dishonoring the flag is not. Similarly, we have upheld reasonable "time, place, or manner" restrictions, but only if they are "justified without reference to the content of the regulated speech." . . .

[T]he exclusion of "fighting words" from the scope of the First Amendment simply means that, for purposes of that Amendment, the unprotected features of the words are, despite their verbal character, essentially a "non-speech" element of communication. Fighting words are thus analogous to a noisy sound truck: Each is, as Justice Frankfurter recognized, a "mode of speech"; both can be used to convey an idea; but neither has, in and of itself, a claim upon the First Amendment. As with the sound truck, however, so also with fighting words: The government may not regulate use based on hostility - or favoritism - towards the underlying message expressed.

. . . . A State might choose to prohibit only that obscenity which is the most patently offensive *in its prurience* - i.e., that which involves the most lascivious displays of sexual activity. But it may not prohibit, for example, only that obscenity which includes offensive political messages. And the Federal Government can criminalize only those threats of violence that are directed against the President -

since the reasons why threats of violence are outside the First Amendment (protecting individuals from the fear of violence, from the disruption that fear engenders, and from the possibility that the threatened violence will occur) have special force when applied to the person of the President. But the Federal Government may not criminalize only those threats against the President that mention his policy on aid to inner cities. And to take a final example, a State may choose to regulate price advertising in one industry but not in others, because the risk of fraud (one of the characteristics of commercial speech that justifies depriving it of full First Amendment protection) is in its view greater there. But a State may not prohibit only that commercial advertising that depicts men in a demeaning fashion.

. . . . A State could, for example, permit all obscene live performances except those involving minors. . . . [S]exually derogatory "fighting words," among other words, may produce a violation of Title VII's general prohibition against sexual discrimination in employment practices. Where the government does not target conduct on the basis of its expressive content, acts are not shielded from regulation merely because they express a discriminatory idea or philosophy.

. . . . [W]e conclude that, even as narrowly construed by the Minnesota Supreme Court, the ordinance is facially [on its surface] unconstitutional. Although the phrase in the ordinance, "arouses anger, alarm or resentment in others," has been limited by the Minnesota Supreme Court's construction to reach only those symbols or displays that amount to "fighting words," the remaining, unmodified terms make clear that the ordinance applies only to "fighting words" that insult, or provoke violence, "on the basis of race, color, creed, religion or gender." Displays containing abusive invective, no matter how vicious or severe, are permissible unless they are addressed to one of the specified disfavored topics. Those who wish to use "fighting words" in connection with other ideas - to express hostility, for example, on the basis of political affiliation, union membership, or homosexuality - are not covered. The First Amendment does not permit St. Paul to impose special prohibitions on those speakers who express views on disfavored subjects.

In its practical operation, moreover, the ordinance goes even beyond mere content discrimination, to actual viewpoint discrimination. Displays containing some words - odious racial epithets, for example - would be prohibited to proponents of all views. But "fighting words" that do not themselves invoke race, color, creed, religion, or gender - aspersions upon a person's mother, for example - would seemingly be usable . . . in the placards of those arguing *in favor* of racial, color, etc. tolerance and equality, but could not be used by that speaker's opponents. One could hold up a sign saying, for example, that all "anti-Catholic bigots" are misbegotten; but not that all "papists" are, for that wold insult and provoke violence "on the basis of religion." St. Paul has no such authority to license one side of a debate to fight freestyle, while requiring the other to follow the Marquis of Queensbury Rules.

What we have here, it must be emphasized, is not a prohibition of fighting words that are directed at certain persons or groups (which would be *facially* valid if it met the requirements of the Equal Protection Clause); but rather, a prohibition of fighting words that contain (as the Minnesota Supreme Court repeatedly emphasized) messages of "bias-motivated" hatred and in particular, as applied to this case, messages "based on virulent notions of racial supremacy." One must wholeheartedly agree with the Minnesota Supreme Court that "[i]t is the responsibility, even the obligation, of diverse communities to confront such notions in whatever form they appear," but the manner of that confrontation cannot consist of selective limitations upon speech. St. Paul . . . asserts that a general "fighting words" law would not meet the city's needs because only a content-specific measure can communicate to minority groups that the "group hatred" aspect of such speech "is not condoned by the majority." The point of the First Amendment is that majority preferences must be expressed in some fashion other than silencing speech on the basis of its content.

. . . . What makes the anger, fear, sense of dishonor, etc. produced by violation of this ordinance distinct from the anger, fear, sense of dishonor, etc. produced by other fighting words is nothing other than the fact that it is caused by a distinctive idea, conveyed by a distinctive message. The First Amendment cannot be evaded that easily. It is obvious that the symbols which will arouse "anger, alarm or resentment in others on the basis of race, color, creed, religion or gender" are those symbols that communicate a message of hostility based on one of these characteristics. St. Paul concedes . . . that the ordinance applies only to "racial, religious, or gender-specific symbols" such as "a burning cross, Nazi swastika or other instrumentality of like import." Indeed, St. Paul argued in the Juvenile Court that "[t]he burning of a cross does express a message and it is, in fact, the content of that message which the St. Paul Ordinance attempts to legislate."

The content-based discrimination reflected in the St. Paul ordinance comes within neither any of the specific exceptions to the First Amendment prohibition we discussed earlier, nor within a more general exception for content discrimination that does not threaten censorship of ideas. It assuredly does not fall within the exception for content discrimination based on the very reasons why the particular class of speech at issue (here, fighting words) is proscribable. . . . St. Paul has not singled out an especially offensive mode of expression - it has not, for example, selected for prohibition only those fighting words that communicate ideas in a threatening (as opposed to a merely obnoxious) manner. Rather, it has proscribed fighting words of whatever manner that communicate messages of racial, gender, or religious intolerance. Selectivity of this sort creates the possibility that the city is seeking to handicap the expression of particular ideas. That possibility would alone be enough to render the ordinance presumptively invalid, but St. Paul's comments and concessions in this case elevate the possibility to a certainty.

. . . . St. Paul . . . defend[s] the conclusion of the Minnesota Supreme Court that, even if the ordinance regulates expression based on hostility towards its protected ideological content, this discrimination is nonetheless justified because it is narrowly tailored to serve compelling state interests. Specifically, they assert that the ordinance helps to ensure the basic human rights of members of groups that have historically been subjected to discrimination, including the right of such group members to live in peace where they wish. We do not doubt that these interests are compelling, and that the ordinance can be said to promote them. But the "danger of censorship" presented by a facially content-based statute requires that that weapon be employed only where it is "*necessary* to serve the asserted [compelling] interest." ... The dispositive question in this case ... is whether content discrimination is reasonably necessary to achieve St. Paul's compelling interests; it plainly is not. An ordinance not limited to the favored topics, for example, would have precisely the same beneficial effect. In fact the only interest distinctively served by the content limitation is that of displaying the city council's special hostility towards the particular biases thus singled out. That is precisely what the First Amendment forbids. The politicians of St. Paul are entitled to express that hostility - but not through the means of imposing unique limitations upon speakers who (however benightedly) disagree.

Let there be no mistake about our belief that burning a cross in someone's front yard is reprehensible. But St. Paul has sufficient means at its disposal to prevent such behavior without adding the First Amendment to the fire.

The judgment of the Minnesota Supreme Court is reversed, and the case is remanded [sent back to that court] for proceedings not inconsistent with this opinion.

HATE CRIMES

Wisconsin v. Mitchell

If a person . . . intentionally selects a person against whom a crime is committed . . . because of race, religion, color, disability, sexual orientation, national origin or ancestry of that person . . . the penalties for the underlying crime are increased.

Wisconsin Hate Crime Punishment Law

On the night of October 7, 1989 in Kenosha, Wisconsin, Todd Mitchell, a black male, instigated and participated, with others, in the severe beating of a young white male. Prior to the beating, Mitchell had said to the group: "Do you all feel hyped up to move on some white people?" And, upon sighting the victim, he had said: "You want to fuck somebody up? There goes a white boy; go get him."

Mitchell was convicted in Kenosha County Circuit Court of aggravated battery, which ordinarily carries a maximum penalty of two years' imprisonment. In 1989 Wisconsin had enacted a penalty enhancement statute to increase the punishment for persons convicted of hate crimes on the basis of race, religion, color, disability, sexual orientation, national origin, or ancestry. Because the jury found that Mitchell had intentionally selected his victim because of race, the maximum sentence was increased to seven years. Mitchell appealed the penalty enhancement as a violation of his First Amendment rights. The Wisconsin Court of Appeals rejected this argument. The Wisconsin Supreme Court, finding the statute violated the First Amendment, reversed his penalty. Wisconsin appealed to the U.S. Supreme Court.

Oral arguments commenced April 21, 1993. On June 11, 1993 Chief Justice William Rehnquist announced the decision of the Court. The edited text follows.

THE MITCHELL COURT

Chief Justice William Rehnquist
Appointed Chief Justice by President Reagan
Appointed Associate Justice by President Nixon
Served 1971 -

Associate Justice Byron White
Appointed by President Kennedy
Served 1962 - 1993

Associate Justice Harry Blackmun
Appointed by President Nixon
Served 1970 -

Associate Justice John Paul Stevens
Appointed by President Ford
Served 1975 -

Associate Justice Sandra Day O'Connor
Appointed by President Reagan
Served 1981 -

Associate Justice Antonin Scalia
Appointed by President Reagan
Served 1986 -

Associate Justice Anthony Kennedy
Appointed by President Reagan
Served 1988 -

Associate Justice David Souter
Appointed by President Bush
Served 1991 -

Associate Justice Clarence Thomas
Appointed by President Bush
Served 1991 -

The unedited text of *Wisconsin v. Mitchell* can be found
in volume 505 of *United States Reports.*

WISCONSIN v. MITCHELL
JUNE 11, 1993

CHIEF JUSTICE REHNQUIST: Respondent Todd Mitchell's sentence for aggravated battery [unlawful assault] was enhanced because he intentionally selected his victim on account of the victim's race. The question presented in this case is whether this penalty enhancement is prohibited by the First and Fourteenth Amendments. We hold that it is not.

On the evening of October 7, 1989, a group of young black men and boys, including Mitchell, gathered at an apartment complex in Kenosha, Wisconsin. Several members of the group discussed a scene from the motion picture "Mississippi Burning," in which a white man beat a young black boy who was praying. The group moved outside and Mitchell asked them: "'Do you all feel hyped up to move on some white people?'" Shortly thereafter, a young white boy approached the group on the opposite side of the street where they were standing. As the boy walked by, Mitchell said: "'You all want to fuck somebody up? There goes a white boy; go get him.'" Mitchell counted to three and pointed in the boy's direction. The group ran towards the boy, beat him severely, and stole his tennis shoes. The boy was rendered unconscious and remained in a coma for four days.

After a jury trial in the Circuit Court for Kenosha County, Mitchell was convicted of aggravated battery. That offense ordinarily carries a maximum sentence of two years' imprisonment. But because the jury found that Mitchell had intentionally selected his victim because of the boy's race, the maximum sentence for Mitchell's offense was increased to seven years under [Wisconsin law]. That [law]

enhances the maximum penalty for an offense whenever
the defendant [the accused] "[i]ntentionally selects the
person against whom the crime . . . is committed . . . because of the race, religion, color, disability, sexual orientation, national origin or ancestry of that person. . . ." The
Circuit Court sentenced Mitchell to four years' imprisonment for the aggravated battery.

Mitchell unsuccessfully sought postconviction relief in the
Circuit Court. Then he appealed his conviction and sentence, challenging the constitutionality of Wisconsin's
penalty-enhancement provision on First Amendment
grounds. The Wisconsin Court of Appeals rejected Mitchell's challenge, but the Wisconsin Supreme Court reversed.
The Supreme Court held that the statute "violates the
First Amendment directly by punishing what the legislature has deemed to be offensive thought." It rejected the
State's contention "that the statute punishes only the
'conduct' of intentional selection of a victim." According
to the court, "[t]he statute punishes the 'because of' aspect
of the defendant's selection, the *reason* the defendant selected the victim, the *motive* behind the selection." And
under *R.A.V. v. St. Paul*, "the Wisconsin legislature cannot
criminalize bigoted thought with which it disagrees."

. . . . We granted certiorari [agreed to hear the case]. . . .
We reverse.

Mitchell argues that we are bound by the Wisconsin Supreme Court's conclusion that the statute punishes bigoted
thought and not conduct. There is no doubt that we are
bound by a state court's construction of a state statute. In
Terminiello, for example, the Illinois courts had defined
the term "'breach of the peace,'" in a city ordinance prohibiting disorderly conduct, to include "'stirs the public to

anger . . . or creates a disturbance.'" We held this construction to be binding on us. But here the Wisconsin Supreme Court did not, strictly speaking, construe the Wisconsin statute in the sense of defining the meaning of a particular statutory word or phrase. Rather, it merely characterized the "practical effect" of the statute for First Amendment purposes. This assessment does not bind us. Once any ambiguities as to the meaning of the statute are resolved, we may form our own judgment as to its operative effect.

The State argues that the statute does not punish bigoted thought, as the Supreme Court of Wisconsin said, but instead punishes only conduct. While this argument is literally correct, it does not dispose of Mitchell's First Amendment challenge. To be sure, our cases reject the "view that an apparently limitless variety of conduct can be labeled 'speech' whenever the person engaging in the conduct intends thereby to express an idea." Thus, a physical assault is not by any stretch of the imagination expressive conduct protected by the First Amendment.

But the fact remains that under the Wisconsin statute the same criminal conduct may be more heavily punished if the victim is selected because of his race or other protected status than if no such motive obtained. Thus, although the statute punishes criminal conduct, it enhances the maximum penalty for conduct motivated by a discriminatory point of view more severely than the same conduct engaged in for some other reason or for no reason at all. Because the only reason for the enhancement is [Mitchell's] discriminatory motive for selecting his victim, [he] argues (and the Wisconsin Supreme Court held) that

the statute violates the First Amendment by punishing offenders' bigoted beliefs.

Traditionally, sentencing judges have considered a wide
variety of factors in addition to evidence bearing on guilt
in determining what sentence to impose on a convicted defendant. The defendant's motive for committing the offense is one important factor. Thus, in many States the
commission of a murder, or other capital offense, for pecuniary gain is a separate aggravating circumstance under
the capital-sentencing statute.

But it is equally true that a defendant's abstract beliefs,
however obnoxious to most people, may not be taken into
consideration by a sentencing judge. In *Dawson*, the State
introduced evidence at a capital-sentencing hearing that
the defendant was a member of a white supremacist prison gang. Because "the evidence proved nothing more than
[the defendant's] abstract beliefs," we held that its admission violated the defendant's First Amendment rights. In
so holding, however, we emphasized that "the Constitution
does not erect a *per se* barrier to the admission of evidence concerning one's beliefs and associations at sentencing simply because those beliefs and associations are protected by the First Amendment." Thus, in *Barclay v. Flor-
ida*, we allowed the sentencing judge to take into account
the defendant's racial animus towards his victim. The evidence in that case showed that the defendant's membership in the Black Liberation Army and desire to provoke
a "race war" were related to the murder of a white man
for which he was convicted. Because "the elements of racial hatred in [the] murder" were relevant to several aggravating factors, we held that the trial judge permissibly
took this evidence into account in sentencing the defendant to death.

. . . . [M]otive plays the same role under the Wisconsin statute as it does under federal and state antidiscrimination laws, which we have previously upheld against constitutional challenge. Title VII, for example, makes it unlawful for an employer to discriminate against an employee "*because of* such individual's race, color, religion, sex, or national origin." . . .

. . . *R.A.V.* . . . involved a First Amendment challenge to a municipal ordinance prohibiting the use of "'fighting words' that insult, or provoke violence, 'on the basis of race, color, creed, religion or gender.'" Because the ordinance only proscribed a class of "fighting words" deemed particularly offensive by the city - *i.e.*, those "that contain . . . messages of 'bias-motivated' hatred" - we held that it violated the rule against content-based discrimination. But whereas the ordinance struck down in *R.A.V.* was explicitly directed at expression (*i.e.*, "speech" or "messages"), the statute in this case is aimed at conduct unprotected by the First Amendment.

Moreover, the Wisconsin statute singles out for enhancement bias-inspired conduct because this conduct is thought to inflict greater individual and societal harm. For example, according to the State . . . , bias-motivated crimes are more likely to provoke retaliatory crimes, inflict distinct emotional harms on their victims, and incite community unrest. The State's desire to redress these perceived harms provides an adequate explanation for its penalty-enhancement provision over and above mere disagreement with offenders' beliefs or biases. As Blackstone said long ago, "it is but reasonable that among crimes of different natures those should be most severely punished, which are the most destructive of the public safety and happiness."

.... The First Amendment ... does not prohibit the evidentiary use of speech to establish the elements of a crime or to prove motive or intent. Evidence of a defendant's previous declarations or statements is commonly admitted in criminal trials subject to evidentiary rules dealing with relevancy, reliability, and the like. Nearly half a century ago, in *Haupt v. United States*, we rejected a contention similar to that advanced by Mitchell here. Haupt was tried for the offense of treason, which, as defined by the Constitution (Art. III, Section 3), may depend very much on proof of motive. To prove that the acts in question were committed out of "adherence to the enemy" rather than "parental solicitude," the Government introduced evidence of conversations that had taken place long prior to the indictment, some of which consisted of statements showing Haupt's sympathy with Germany and Hitler and hostility towards the United States. We rejected Haupt's argument that this evidence was improperly admitted. While "[s]uch testimony is to be scrutinized with care to be certain the statements are not expressions of mere lawful and permissible difference of opinion with our own government or quite proper appreciation of the land of birth," we held that "these statements ... clearly were admissible on the question of intent and adherence to the enemy."

For the foregoing reasons, we hold that Mitchell's First Amendment rights were not violated by the application of the Wisconsin penalty-enhancement provision in sentencing him. The judgment of the Supreme Court of Wisconsin is therefore reversed, and the case is remanded [sent back to that court] for further proceedings not inconsistent with this opinion.

THE U.S. CONSTITUTION

PREAMBLE

We the people of the United States, in order to form a more perfect union, establish justice, insure domestic tranquility, provide for the common defense, promote the general welfare, and secure the blessings of liberty to ourselves and our posterity, do ordain and establish this Constitution for the United States of America.

ARTICLE I

Section 1. All legislative powers herein granted shall be vested in a Congress of the United States, which shall consist of a Senate and House of Representatives.

Section 2. (1) The House of Representatives shall be composed of members chosen every second year by the people of several states, and the electors in each state shall have the qualifications requisite for electors of the most numerous branch of the State Legislature.

(2) No person shall be a Representative who shall not have attained to the age of twenty-five years, and been seven years a citizen of the United States, and who shall not, when elected, be an inhabitant of that state in which he shall be chosen.

(3) Representatives and direct taxes shall be apportioned among the several states which may be included within this union, according to their respective numbers, which shall be determined by adding to the whole number of free persons, including those bound to service for a term of years, and excluding Indians not taxed, three-fifths of all other persons. The actual enumeration shall be made

within three years after the first meeting of the Congress
of the United States, and within every subsequent term of
ten years, in such manner as they shall be law direct. The
number of Representatives shall not exceed one for every
thirty thousand, but each state shall have at least one Representative; and until such enumeration shall be made, the
State of New Hampshire shall be entitled to choose three,
Massachusetts eight, Rhode Island and Providence Plantations one, Connecticut five, New York six, New Jersey
four, Pennsylvania eight, Delaware one, Maryland six, Virginia ten, North Carolina five, South Carolina five, and
Georgia three.

(4) When vacancies happen in the representation from
any state, the executive authority thereof shall issue Writs
of Election to fill such vacancies.

(5) The House of Representatives shall choose their
Speaker and other Officers; and shall have the sole power
of impeachment.

Section 3. (1) The Senate of the United States shall be
composed of two Senators from each state, chosen by the
legislature thereof, for six years; and each Senator shall
have one vote.

(2) Immediately after they shall be assembled in consequence of the first election, they shall be divided as equally as may be into three classes. The seats of the Senators
of the first class shall be vacated at the expiration of the
second year, of the second class at the expiration of the
fourth year, and of the third class at the expiration of the
sixth year, so that one-third may be chosen every second
year; and if vacancies happen by resignation, or otherwise,
during the recess of the legislature of any state, the execu-

tive thereof may take temporary appointments until the next meeting of the legislature, which shall then fill such vacancies.

(3) No person shall be a Senator who shall not have attained to the age of thirty years, and been nine years a citizen of the United States, and who shall not, when elected, be an inhabitant of that state for which he shall be chosen.

(4) The Vice President of the United States shall be President of the Senate, but shall have no vote, unless they be equally divided.

(5) The Senate shall choose their other Officers, and also a President pro tempore, in the absence of the Vice President, or when he shall exercise the Office of President of the United States.

(6) The Senate shall have the sole power to try all impeachments. When sitting for that purpose, they shall be on oath or affirmation. When the President of the United States is tried, the Chief Justice shall preside: and no person shall be convicted without the concurrence of two-thirds of the members present.

(7) Judgment in cases of impeachment shall not extend further than to removal from office, and disqualification to hold and enjoy any office of honor, trust, or profit under the United States: but the party convicted shall nevertheless be liable and subject to indictment, trial, judgment, and punishment, according to law.

Section 4. (1) The times, places and manner of holding elections for Senators and Representatives, shall be prescribed in each state by the legislature thereof; but the Congress may at any time by law make or alter such regulations, except as to the places of choosing Senators.

(2) The Congress shall assemble at least once in every year, and such meeting shall be on the first Monday in December, unless they shall by law appoint a different day.

Section 5. (1) Each House shall be the judge of the elections, returns, and qualifications of its own members, and a majority of each shall constitute a quorum to do business; but a smaller number may adjourn from day to day, and may be authorized to compel the attendance of absent members, in such manner, and under such penalties as each House may provide.

(2) Each House may determine the rules of its proceedings, punish its members for disorderly behavior, and, with the concurrence of two-thirds, expel a member.

(3) Each House shall keep a journal of its proceedings, and from time to time publish the same, excepting such parts as may in their judgment require secrecy; and the yeas and nays of the members of either House on any question shall, at the desire of one-fifth of those present, be entered on the journal.

(4) Neither House, during the Session of Congress, shall, without the consent of the other, adjourn for more than three days, nor to any other place than that in which the two Houses shall be sitting.

Section 6. (1) The Senators and Representatives shall receive a compensation for their services, to be ascertained by law, and paid out of the Treasury of the United States. They shall in all cases, except treason, felony and breach of the peace, be privileged from arrest during their attendance at the session of their respective Houses, and in going to and returning from the same; and for any speech or debate in either House, they shall not be questioned in any other place.

(2) No Senator or Representative shall, during the time for which he was elected, be appointed to any civil office under the authority of the United States, which shall have been created, or the emoluments whereof shall have been increased during such time and no person holding any office under the United States, shall be a member of either House during his continuance in office.

Section 7. (1) All bills for raising revenue shall originate in the House of Representatives; but the Senate may propose or concur with amendments as on other bills.

(2) Every bill which shall have passed the House of Representatives and the Senate, shall, before it become a law, be presented to the President of the United States; if he approve he shall sign it, but if not he shall return it, with his objections to the House in which it shall have originated, who shall enter the objections at large on their journal, and proceed to reconsider it. If after such reconsideration two-thirds of that House shall agree to pass the bill, it shall be sent together with the objections, to the other House, by which it shall likewise be reconsidered, and if approved by two-thirds of that House, it shall become a law. But in all such cases the votes of both Houses shall be determined by yeas and nays, and the names of the persons voting for and against the bill shall be entered on the journal of each House respectively. If any bill shall not

be returned by the President within ten days (Sundays excepted) after it shall have been presented to him, the same shall be a law, in like manner as if he had signed it, unless the Congress by their adjournment prevent its return in which case it shall not be a law.

(3) Every order, resolution, of vote, to which the concurrence of the Senate and House of Representatives may be necessary (except on a question of adjournment) shall be presented to the President of the United States; and before the same shall take effect, shall be approved by him, or being disapproved by him, shall be repassed by two-thirds of the Senate and House of Representatives, according to the rules and limitations prescribed in the case of a bill.

Section 8. (1) The Congress shall have the power to lay and collect taxes, duties, imposts and excises, to pay the debts and provide for the common defense and general welfare of the United States; but all duties, imposts and excises shall be uniform throughout the United States;

(2) To borrow money on the credit of the United States;

(3) To regulate commerce with foreign nations, and among the several states, and with the Indian Tribes;

(4) To establish an uniform Rule of Naturalization, and uniform laws on the subject of bankruptcies throughout the United States;

(5) To coin money, regulate the value thereof, and of foreign coin, and fix the standard of weights and measures;

(6) To provide for the punishment of counterfeiting the securities and current coin of the United States;

(7) To establish Post Offices and Post Roads;

(8) To promote the progress of science and useful arts, by securing for limited times to authors and inventors the exclusive right to their respective writings and discoveries;

(9) To constitute tribunals inferior the Supreme Court;

(10) To define and punish piracies and felonies committed on the high seas, and offenses against the Law of Nations;

(11) To declare war, grant Letters of Marque and Reprisal, and make rules concerning captures on land and water;

(12) To raise and support armies, but no appropriation of money to that use shall be for a longer term than two years;

(13) To provide and maintain a Navy;

(14) To make rules for the government and regulation of the land and naval forces;

(15) To provide for calling forth the Militia to execute the laws of the Union, suppress insurrections and repel invasions;

(16) To provide for organizing, arming, and disciplining, the Militia, and for governing such part of them as may be employed in the service of the United States, reserving to the states respectively, the appointment of the Officers,

and the authority of training the Militia according to the discipline prescribed by Congress;

(17) To exercise exclusive legislation in all cases whatsoever, over such district (not exceeding ten miles square) as may, be cession of particular states, and the acceptance of Congress, become the Seat of the Government of the United States, and to exercise like authority over all places purchased by the consent of the legislature of the state in which the same shall be, for the erection of forts, magazines, arsenals, dockyards, and other needful buildings; - and

(18) To make all laws which shall be necessary and proper for carrying into execution the foregoing powers, and all other powers vested by this Constitution in the Government of the United States, or in any Department or Officer thereof.

Section 9. (1) The migration or importation of such persons as any of the states now existing shall think proper to admit, shall not be prohibited by the Congress prior to the year one thousand eight hundred and eight, but a tax or duty may be imposed on such importation, not exceeding ten dollars for each person.

(2) The privilege of the Writ of Habeas Corpus shall not be suspended, unless when in cases of rebellion or invasion the public safety may require it.

(3) No Bill of Attainder or ex post facto law shall be passed.

(4) No capitation, or other direct, tax shall be laid, unless in proportion to the Census or enumeration herein before directed to be taken.

(5) No tax or duty shall be laid on articles exported from any state.

(6) No preference shall be given by any regulation of commerce or revenue to th ports of one state over those of another: nor shall vessels bound to, or from, one state be obliged to enter, clear, or pay duties in another.

(7) No money shall be drawn from the Treasury, but in consequence eof appropriations made by law; and a regular statement and account of the receipts and expenditures of all public money shall be published from time to time.

(8) No title of nobility shall be granted by the United States: and no person holding any office of profit or trust under them, shall, without the consent of the Congress, accept of any present, emolument, office, or title, of any kind whatever, from any King, Prince, or foreign State.

Section 10. (1) No state shall enter into any treaty, alliance, or confederation; grant Letter of Marque and Reprisal; coin money; emit bills of credit; make any thing but gold and silver coin a tender in payment of debts; pass and Bill of Attainder, ex post facto law, or law impairing the obligation of contracts, or grant any title of nobility.

(2) No state shall, without the consent of the Congress, lay any imposts or duties on imports or exports, except what may be absolutely necessary for executing its inspection laws: and the net produce of all duties and imposts, laid by any state on imports or exports, shall be for the use of

the Treasury of the United States; and all such laws shall be subject to the revision and control of the Congress.

(3) No state shall, without the consent of Congress, lay any duty of tonnage, keep troops, or ships of war in time of peace, enter into any agreement or compact with another state, or with a foreign power, or engage in war, unless actually invaded, or in such imminent danger as will not admit of delay.

ARTICLE II

Section 1. (1) The executive power shall be vested in a President of the United States of America. He shall hold his office during the term of four years, and, together with the Vice President, chosen for the same term, be elected, as follows:

(2) Each state shall appoint, in such manner as the legislature thereof may direct, a number of electors, equal to the whole number os Senators and Representatives to which the state may be entitled in the Congress; but no Senator or Representative, or person holding an office of trust or profit under the United States, shall be appointed an Elector.

(3) The Electors shall meet in their respective states, and vote by ballot for two persons, of whom one at least shall not be an inhabitant of the same state with themselves. And they shall make a list of all the persons voted for, and of the number of votes for each; which list they shall sign and certify, and transmit sealed to the Seat of the Government of the United States, directed to the President of the Senate. The President of the Senate shall, in the presence of the Senate and House of Representatives,

open all the certificates, and the votes shall then be counted. The person having the greatest number of votes shall be the President, if such number be a majority of the whole number of Electors appointed; and if there be more than one who have such majority, and have an equal number of votes, then the House of Representatives shall immediately choose by ballot one of them for President; and if no person have a majority, then from the five highest on the list the said House shall in like manner choose the President. But in choosing the President, the votes shall be taken by states the representation from each state having one vote; a quorum for this purpose shall consist of a member or members from two-thirds of the states, and a majority of all the states shall be necessary to a choice. In every case, after the choice of the President, the person having the greater number of votes of the Electors shall be the Vice President. But if there should remain two or more who have equal votes, the Senate shall choose from them by ballot the Vice President.

(4) The Congress may determine the time of choosing the Electors, and the day on which they shall give their votes; which day shall be the same throughout the United States.

(5) No person except a natural born citizen, or a citizen of the United States, at the time of the adoption of this Constitution, shall be eligible to the Office of President; neither shall any person be eligible to that Office who shall not have attained to the age of thirty-five years, and been fourteen years a resident within the United States.

(6) In case of the removal of the President from Office, or of his death, resignation or inability to discharge the powers and duties of the said Office, the same shall devolve on the Vice President, and the Congress may by law

provide for the case of removal, death, resignation of inability, both of the President and Vice President, declaring
what Officer shall then act as President, and such Officer
shall act accordingly, until the disability be removed, or a
President shall be elected.

(7) The President shall, at stated times, receive for his
services, a compensation, which shall neither be increased
nor diminished during the period for which he shall have
been elected, and he shall not receive within that period
any other emolument from the United States, or any of
them.

(8) Before he enter on the execution of his Office, he
shall take the following Oath or Affirmation: "I do solemnly swear (or affirm) that I will faithfully execute the
Office of President of the United States, and will to the
best of my ability, preserve, protect and defend the Constitution of the United States."

Section 2. (1) The President shall be Commander in Chief
of the Army and Navy of the United States, and of the
militia of the several states, when called into the actual
service of the United States; he may require the opinion,
in writing, of the principal Officer in each of the Executive Departments, upon any subject relating to the duties
of their respective Offices, and he shall have power to
grant reprieves and pardons for offenses against the United States, except in cases of impeachment.

(2) He shall have power, by and with the advice and consent of the Senate to make treaties, provided two-thirds of
the Senators present concur; and he shall nominate, and
by and with the advice and consent of the Senate, shall appoint Ambassadors, other public Ministers and Consuls,

Judges of the supreme Court, and all other Officers of the United States, whose appointments are not herein otherwise provided for, and which shall be established by law; but the Congress may be law vest the appointment of such inferior Officers, as they think proper, in the President alone, in the courts of law, or in the Heads of Departments.

(3) The President shall have power to fill up all vacancies that may happen during the recess of the Senate, by granting commissions which shall expire at the end of their next Session.

Section 3. He shall from time to time give to the Congress information of the State of the Union, and recommend to their consideration such measures as he shall judge necessary and expedient; he may, on extraordinary occasions, convene both Houses, or either of them, and in case of disagreement between them, with respect to the time of adjournment, he may adjourn them to such time as he shall think proper; he shall receive Ambassadors and other public Ministers; he shall take care that the laws be faithfully executed, and shall commission all the Officers of the United States.

Section 4. The President, Vice President and all civil Officers of the United States, shall be removed from office on impeachment for, and conviction of, treason, bribery, or other high crimes and misdemeanors.

ARTICLE III

Section 1. The judicial power of the United States, shall be vested in one supreme Court, and in such inferior courts as the Congress may from time to time ordain and establish. The Judges, both of the supreme and inferior courts, shall hold their Offices during good behaviour, and shall, at stated times, receive for their services a compensation, which shall not be diminished during their continuance in office.

Section 2. (1) The judicial power shall extend to all cases, in law and equity, arising under this Constitution, the laws of the United States, and treaties made, or which shall be made, under their authority; – to all cases affecting Ambassadors, other public Ministers and Consuls; – to all cases of admiralty and maritime jurisdiction; – to controversies to which the United States shall be a party; – to controversies between two or more states; – between a state and citizens of another state; – between citizens of different states; – between citizens of the same state claiming lands under the grants of different states, and between a state, or the citizens thereof, and foreign states, citizens or subjects.

(2) In all cases affecting Ambassadors, other public Ministers and Consuls, and those in which a state shall be a party, the supreme Court shall have original jurisdiction. In all the other cases before mentioned, the supreme Court shall have appellate jurisdiction, both as to law and fact, with such exceptions, and under such regulations as the Congress shall make.

(3) The trial of all crimes, except in cases of impeachment, shall be by jury; and such trial shall be held in the state where the said crimes shall have been committed; but when not committed within any state, the trial shall be at such place or places as the Congress may be law have directed.

Section 3. (1) Treason against the United States, shall consist only in levying war against them, or, in adhering to their enemies, giving them aid and comfort. No person shall be convicted of treason unless on the testimony of two witnesses to the same overt act, or on confession in open Court.

(2) The Congress shall have power to declare the punishment of treason, but no Attainder of Treason shall work corruption of blood, or forfeiture except during the life of the person attainted.

ARTICLE IV

Section 1. Full faith and credit shall be given in each state to the public acts, records, and judicial proceedings of every other state. And the Congress may by general laws prescribe the manner in which such acts, records and proceedings shall be proved, and the effect thereof.

Section 2. (1) The citizens of each state shall be entitled to all privileges and immunities of citizens in the several states.

(2) A person charged in any state with treason, felony, or other crime, who shall flee from justice, and be found in another state, shall on demand of the executive authority of the state from which he fled, be delivered up, to be removed to the state having jurisdiction of the crime.

(3) No person held to service or labour in one state, under the laws thereof, escaping into another, shall, in consequence of any law or regulation therein, be discharged from such service or labour, but shall be delivered up on

claim of the party to whom such service or labour may be due.

Section 3. (1) New states may be admitted by the Congress into this Union; but no new state shall be formed or erected within the jurisdiction of any other state; nor any state be formed by the junction of two or more states, or parts of states, without the consent of the legislatures of the states concerned as well as of the Congress.

(2) The Congress shall have power to dispose of and make all needful rules and regulations respecting the territory or other property belonging to the United States; and nothing in this Constitution shall be so construed as to prejudice any claims of the United States, or of any particular state.

Section 4. The United States shall guarantee to every state in this Union a Republican form of government, and shall protect each of them against invasion; and on application of the Legislature, or of the Executive (when the Legislature cannot be convened) against domestic violence.

ARTICLE V

The Congress, whenever two-thirds of both Houses shall deem it necessary, shall propose amendments to this Constitution, or, on the application of the Legislatures of two-thirds of the several states, shall call a convention for proposing amendments, which, in either case, shall be valid to all intents and purposes, as part of this constitution, when ratified by the Legislatures of three-fourths of the several states, or by conventions in three-fourths thereof, as the one or the other mode of ratification may be proposed by the Congress; provided that no amendment which may be made prior to the year one thousand eight hundred and eight shall in any manner affect the first and fourth clauses in the Ninth Section of the first Article; and that no state, without its consent, shall be deprived of its equal suffrage in the Senate.

ARTICLE VI

(1) All debts contracted and engagements entered into, before the adoption of this Constitution shall be as valid against the United States under this Constitution, as under the Confederation.

(2) This Constitution, and the laws of the United States which shall be made in pursuance thereof; and all treaties made, or which shall be made, under the authority of the United States, shall be the supreme law of the land; and the Judges in every state shall be bound thereby, any thing in the Constitution or laws of any state to the contrary notwithstanding.

(3) The Senators and Representatives before mentioned, and the Members of the several State Legislatures, and all executive and judicial Officers, both of the United States and of the several states, shall be bound by oath or affirmation, to support this Constitution; but no religious test shall ever be required as a qualification to any Office or public trust under the United States.

ARTICLE VII

The ratification of the Conventions of nine states shall be sufficient for the establishment of this Constitution between the states so ratifying the same.

AMENDMENT I (1791)

Congress shall make no law respecting an establishment of religion, or prohibiting the free exercise thereof; or abridging the freedom of speech, or of the press; or the right of the people peaceably to assemble, and to petition the Government for a redress of grievances.

AMENDMENT II (1791)

A well regulated Militia, being necessary to the security of a free State, the right of the people to keep and bear arms, shall not be infringed.

AMENDMENT III (1791)

No soldier shall, in time of peace be quartered in any house, without the consent of the owner, nor in time of war, but in a manner to be prescribed by law.

AMENDMENT IV (1791)

The right of the people to be secure in their persons, houses, papers, and effects, against unreasonable searches and seizures, shall not be violated, and no warrants shall issue, but upon probable cause, supported by oath or affirmation, and particularly describing the place to be searched, and the persons or things to be seized.

AMENDMENT V (1791)

No person shall be held to answer for a capital, or otherwise infamous crime, unless on a presentment or indictment of a Grand Jury, except in cases arising in the land or naval forces, or in the Militia, when in actual service in time of war or public danger; nor shall any person be subject for the same offense to be twice put in jeopardy of life or limb; nor shall be compelled in any criminal case to be a witness against himself, nor be deprived of life, liberty, or property, without due process of law; nor shall private property be taken for public use, without just compensation.

AMENDMENT VI (1791)

In all criminal prosecutions, the accused shall enjoy the right to a speedy and public trial, by an impartial jury of the state and district wherein the crime shall have been committed, which district shall have been previously ascertained by law, and to be informed of the nature and cause of the accusation; to be confronted with the witnesses against him; to have compulsory process for obtaining witnesses in his favor, and to have the assistance of counsel for his defense.

AMENDMENT VII (1791)

In suits at common law, where the value in controversy shall exceed twenty dollars, the right of trial by jury shall be preserved, and no fact tried by jury, shall be otherwise re-examined in any Court of the United States, than according to the rules of the common law.

AMENDMENT VIII (1791)

Excessive bail shall not be required, nor excessive fines imposed, nor cruel and unusual punishments inflicted.

AMENDMENT IX (1791)

The enumeration in the Constitution, of certain rights, shall not be construed to deny or disparage others retained by the people.

AMENDMENT X (1791)

The powers not delegated to the United States by the Constitution, nor prohibited by it to the States, are reserved to the States respectively, or to the people.

AMENDMENT XI (1798)

The judicial power of the United States shall not be construed to extend to any suit in law or equity, commenced or prosecuted against one of the United States by citizens of another state, or by citizens or subjects of any foreign state.

AMENDMENT XII (1804)

The Electors shall meet in their respective states and vote by ballot for President and Vice-President, one of whom, at least, shall not be an inhabitant of the same stat with themselves; they shall name in their ballots the person voted for as President, and in distinct ballots the person voted for as Vice-President, and they shall make distinct lists of all persons voted for as President, and of all persons voted for as Vice-President, and of the number of votes for each, which lists they shall sign and certify, and transmit sealed to the seat of the government of the United States, directed to the President of the Senate; – the President of the Senate shall, in the presence of the Senate and House of Representatives, open all the certificates and the votes shall then be counted; — the person having the greatest number of votes for President, shall be the President, if such number be a majority of the persons having the highest numbers not exceeding three on the list of those voted for as President, the House of Representatives shall choose immediately, by ballot, the President. But in choosing the President, the votes shall be taken by states, the representation from each state having one vote; a quorum for his purpose shall consist of a member or members from two-thirds of the states, and a majority of all the states shall be necessary to a choice. And if the House of Representatives shall not choose a President whenever the right of choice shall devolve upon them before the fourth day of March next following, then the Vice-President shall act as President, as in the case of the death or other constitutional disability of the President. — The person having the greatest number of votes as Vice-President, shall be the Vice-President, if such number be a majority of the whole number of Electors appointed, and if no person have a majority, then from the two highest numbers on the list, the Senate shall choose the Vice-President; a quorum for the purpose shall consist of two-thirds of the whole number of Senators, and a majority of the whole number shall be necessary to a choice. But no person constitutionally ineligible to the office of President shall be eligible to that of Vice-President of the United States.

AMENDMENT XIII (1865)

Section 1. Neither slavery nor involuntary servitude, except as a punishment for crime whereof the party shall have been duly convicted, shall exist within the United States, or any place subject to their jurisdiction.

Section 2. Congress shall have power to enforce this article by appropriate legislation.

AMENDMENT XIV (1868)

Section 1. All persons born or naturalized in the United States, and subject to the jurisdiction thereof, are citizens of the United States and of the state wherein they reside. No state shall make or enforce any law which shall abridge the privileges or immunities of citizens of the United States; nor shall any state deprive any person of life, liberty, or property, without due process of law; nor deny to any person within its jurisdiction the equal protection of the laws.

Section 2. Representatives shall be apportioned among the several states according to their respective numbers, counting the whole number of persons in each State excluding Indians not taxed. But when the right to vote at any election for the choice of electors for President and Vice President of the United States, Representatives in Congress, the Executive and Judicial officers of a state, or the members of the Legislature thereof, is denied to any of the male inhabitants of such state, being twenty-one years of age, and citizens of the United States, or in any way abridged, except for participation in rebellion, or other crime, the basis of representation therein shall be reduced in the proportion which the number of such male citizens shall bear to the whole number of male citizens twenty-one years of age in such state.

Section 3. No person shall be a Senator or Representative in Congress, or elector of President and Vice President, or hold any office, civil or military, under the United States, or under any state, who having previously taken an oath, as a member of Congress, or as an officer of the United States, or as a member of any state legislature, or as an executive or judicial officer of any state, to support the Constitution of the United States, shall have engaged in insurrection or rebellion against the same, or given aid or comfort to the enemies thereof. But Congress may by a vote of two-thirds of each House, remove such disability.

Section 4. The validity of the public debt of the United States, authorized by law, including debts incurred for payment of pensions and bounties for services in suppressing insurrection or rebellion, shall not be questioned. But neither the United States nor any state shall assume or pay any debt or obligation incurred in aid of insurrection or rebellion against the United States, or any claim for the loss or emancipation of any slave; but all such debts, obligations and claims shall be held illegal and void.

Section 5. The Congress shall have power to enforce, by appropriate legislation, the provisions of this article.

AMENDMENT XV (1870)

Section 1. The right of citizens of the United States to vote shall not be denied or abridged by the United States or by any state on account of race, color, or previous condition of servitude.

Section 2. The Congress shall have power to enforce this article by appropriate legislation.

AMENDMENT XVI (1913)

The Congress shall have power to lay and collect taxes on income, from whatever source derived, without apportionment among the several states, and without regard to any census or enumeration.

AMENDMENT XVII (1913)

(1) The Senate of the United States shall be composed of two Senators from each state, elected by the people thereof, for six years; and each Senator shall have one vote. The electors in each State shall have the qualifications requisite for electors of the most numerous branch of the state legislatures.

(2) When vacancies happen in the representation of any state in the Senate, the executive authority of such state shall issue writs of election to fill such vacancies: *provided*, that the legislature of any state may empower the executive thereof to make temporary appointments until the people fill the vacancies by election as the legislature may direct.

(3) This amendment shall not be so construed as to affect the election or term of any Senator chosen before it becomes valid as part of the Constitution.

AMENDMENT XVIII (1919)

Section 1. After one year from the ratification of this article the manufacture, sale, or transportation of intoxicating liquors within, the importation thereof into, or the exportation thereof from the United States and all territory subject to the jurisdiction thereof for beverage purposes is hereby prohibited.

Section 2. The Congress and the several states shall have concurrent power to enforce this article by appropriate legislation.

Section 3. This article shall be inoperative unless it shall have been ratified as an amendment to the Constitution by the legislatures of the several states, as provided in the Constitution, within seven years from the date of the submission hereof to the states by the Congress.

AMENDMENT XIX (1920)

(1) The right of citizens of the United States to vote shall not be denied or abridged by the United States or by any state on account of sex.

(2) Congress shall have power to enforce this article by appropriate legislation.

AMENDMENT XX (1933)

Section 1. The terms of the President and Vice President shall end at noon on the 20th day of January, and the terms of Senators and Representatives at noon on the 3d day of January, of the years in which such terms would have ended if this article had not been ratified; and the terms of their successors shall then begin.

Section 2. The Congress shall assemble at least once in every year, and such meeting shall begin at noon on the 3d day of January, unless they shall by law appoint a different day.

Section 3. If, at the time fixed for the beginning of the term of the President, the President elect shall have died, the Vice President elect shall become President. If the President shall not have been chosen before the time fixed for the beginning of his term, or if the President elect shall have failed to qualify, then the Vice President elect shall act as President until a President shall have qualified; and the Congress may by law provide for the case wherein neither a President elect nor a Vice President elect shall have qualified, declaring who shall then act as President, or the manner in which one who is to act shall be selected, and such person shall act accordingly until a President or Vice President shall have qualified.

Section 4. The Congress may by law provide for the case of the death of any of the persons from whom the House of Representatives may choose a President whenever the right of choice shall have devolved upon them, and for the case of the death of any of the persons from whom the Senate may choose a Vice President whenever the right of choice shall have devolved upon them.

Section 5. Sections 1 and 2 shall take effect on the 15th day of October following the ratification of this article.

Section 6. This article shall be inoperative unless it shall have been ratified as an amendment to the Constitution by the legislatures of three-fourths of the several states within seven years from the date of its submission.

AMENDMENT XXI (1933)

Section 1. The eighteenth article of amendment to the Constitution of the United States is hereby repealed.

Section 2. The transportation or importation into any state, territory, or possession of the United States for delivery or use therein of intoxicating liquors, in violation of the laws thereof, is hereby prohibited.

Section 3. This article shall be inoperative unless it shall have been ratified as an amendment to the Constitution by conventions in the several states, as provided in the Constitution, within seven years from the date of the submission hereof to the states by the Congress.

AMENDMENT XXII (1951)

Section 1. No person shall be elected to the office of the President more than twice, and no person who has held the office of President, or acted as President, for more than two ears of a term to which some other person was elected President shall be elected to the office of President more than once. But this Article shall not apply to any person holding the office of President when this Article was proposed by the Congress, and shall not prevent any person who may be holding the office of President, or acting as President, during the term within which this Article becomes operative from holding the office of President or acting as President during the remainder of such term.

Section 2. This article shall be inoperative unless it shall have been ratified as an amendment to the Constitution by the legislatures of three-fourths of the several states within seven years from the date of its submission to the states by the Congress.

AMENDMENT XXIII (1961)

Section 1. The District constituting the seat of Government of the United States shall appoint in such manner as the Congress may direct:

A number of electors of President and Vice President equal to the whole number of Senators and Representatives in Congress to which the District would be entitled if it were a state, but in no event more than the least populous state; they shall be in addition to those appointed by the states, but they shall be considered, for the purposes of the election of President and Vice President, to be electors appointed by a state; and they shall meet in the District and perform such duties as provided by the twelfth article of amendment.

Section 2. The Congress shall have power to enforce this article by appropriate legislation.

AMENDMENT XXIV (1964)

Section 1. The right of citizens of the United States to vote in any primary or other election for President or Vice President, for electors for President or Vice President, or for Senator or Representative in Congress, shall not be denied or abridged by the United States, or any state by reason of failure to pay any poll tax or other tax.

Section 2. The Congress shall have power to enforce this article by appropriate legislation.

AMENDMENT XXV (1967)

Section 1. In case of the removal of the President from office or of his death or resignation, the Vice President shall become President.

Section 2. Whenever there is a vacancy in the office of the Vice President, the President shall nominate a Vice President who shall take office upon confirmation by a majority vote of both Houses of Congress.

Section 3. Whenever the President transmits to the President pro tempore of the Senate and the Speaker of the House of Representatives his written declaration that he is unable to discharge the powers and duties of his office, and until he transmits to them a written declaration to the contrary, such powers and duties shall be discharged by the Vice President as Acting President.

Section 4. Whenever the Vice President and a majority of either the principal officers of the executive departments or of such other body as Congress may by law provide, transmit to the President pro tempore of the Senate and the Speaker of the House of Representatives their written declaration that the President is unable to discharge the powers and duties of his office, the Vice President shall immediately assume the powers and duties of the office as Acting President.

Thereafter, when the President transmits to the President pro tempore of the Senate and the Speaker of the House of Representatives his written declaration that no inability exists, he shall resume the powers and duties of his office unless the Vice President and a majority of either the principal officers of the executive department or of such

other body as Congress may by law provide, transmit
within four days to the President pro tempore of the Senate and the Speaker of the House of Representatives their
written declaration and the President is unable to discharge the powers and duties of his office. Thereupon
Congress shall decide the issue, assembling within forty-
eight hours for that purpose if not in session. If the Congress, within twenty-one days after receipt of the latter
written declaration, or, if Congress is not in session, within twenty-one days after Congress is required to assemble,
determines by two-thirds vote of both Houses that the
President is unable to discharge the power and duties of
his office, the Vice President shall continue to discharge
the same as Acting President; otherwise, the President
shall resume the powers and duties of his office.

AMENDMENT XXVI (1971)

Section 1. The right of citizens of the United States, who
are eighteen years of age or older, to vote shall not be denied or abridged by the United States or by any state on
account of age.

Section 2. The Congress shall have power to enforce this
article by appropriate legislation.

AMENDMENT XXVII (1992)

No law, varying the compensation for the services of the
Senators and Representatives, shall take effect, until an
election of Representatives shall have intervened.

BIBLIOGRAPHY

FEDERAL SUPREMACY

Gunther, Gerald, Editor, *John Marshall's Defense of McCulloch v. Maryland*, Stanford, CA: Stanford University Press, 1969.

Remini, Robert V., *Andrew Jackson and the Bank War: A Study in the Growth of Presidential Power*, New York, NY: Norton, 1967.

THE TRAIL OF TEARS

Anderson, William L., Editor, *Cherokee Removal: Before and After*, Athens, GA: University of Georgia Press, 1991.

Ehle, John, *Trail of Tears: The Rise and Fall of the Cherokee Nation*, New York, NY: Doubleday, 1988.

Filler, Louis, *The Removal of the Cherokee Nation: Manifest Destiny or National Dishonor?*, Boston, MA: Heath, 1966.

Lumpkin, Wilson, *The Removal of the Cherokee Indians from Georgia*, New York, NY: Arno Press, 1969.

Parker, Thomas V., *The Cherokee Indians, with Special Reference to their Relations With the United States Government*, New York: Grafton Press, 1907.

LINCOLN'S SUSPENSION OF HABEAS CORPUS

Duker, William F., *A Constitutional History of Habeas Corpus*, Westport, CT: Greenwood Press, 1980.

Klaus, Samuel, Editor, *The Milligan Case*, New York, NY: Da Capo Press, 1970.

Neely, Mark E., *The Fate of Liberty: Abraham Lincoln and Civil Liberties*, New York, NY: Oxford University Press, 1991.

SEPARATE BUT EQUAL

Lofgren, Charles A., *The Plessy Case: A Legal-Historical Interpretation*, New York, NY: Oxford University Press, 1987.

Olsen, Otto H., *The Thin Disguise: Turning Point in Negro History; Plessy v. Ferguson: A Documentary Presentation, 1864-1896*, New York, NY: Humanities Press, 1967.

TRUST BUSTING

Bringhurst, Bruce, *Antitrust and the Oil Monopoly: The Standard Oil Cases, 1890-1911*, Westport, CT: Greenwood Press, 1979.

Lloyd, Henry D., *Wealth Against Commonwealth*,
Englewood Cliffs, NJ: Prentice-Hall, 1963.

Manning, Thomas G., *The Standard Oil Company: The
Rise of a National Monopoly*, New York, NY: Holt,
Rinehart & Winston, 1964.

CHILD LABOR

Fuller, Raymond G., *Child Labor and the Constitution*,
New York, NY: Thomas Y. Cromwell, 1923.

Stein, R. Conrad, *The Story of Child Labor Laws*, Chicago,
IL: Children's Press, 1984.

THE ATOMIC SPIES

Root, Jonathan, *The Betrayers: The Rosenberg Case - A
Reappraisal of an American Crisis*, New York, NY:
Coward-McCann, 1963.

Wexley, John, *The Judgment of Julius and Ethel
Rosenberg*, New York, NY: Cameron & Kahn, 1955.

LIBEL

Hemmer, Joseph J., *The Supreme Court and the First
Amendment*, New York, NY: Random House, 1991.

Lewis, Anthony, *Make No Law: The Sullivan Case and the
First Amendment*, New York, NY: Random House, 1991.

Schwartz, Bernard, *Freedom of the Press*, New York, NY: Facts on File, 1992.

CONSCIENTIOUS OBJECTION

Ali, Muhammad, *The Greatest: My Own Story*, New York, NY: Random House, 1975.

Conklin, Thomas, *Muhammad Ali: The Fight for Respect*, Brookfield, CT: Millbrook Press, 1991.

Schlissel, Lillian, *Conscience in America: A Documentary History of Conscientious Objection in America, 1757-1967*, New York, NY: Dutton, 1968.

HATE CRIMES

Matsuda, Mari J., Editor, *Words That Wound: Critical Race Theory, Assaultive Speech, and the First Amendment*, Boulder, CO: Westview Press, 1993.

Newton, Michael, and Judy Ann Newton, *Racial and Religious Violence in America: A Chronology*, New York, NY: Garland, 1991.

THE SUPREME COURT

Agresto, John, *The Supreme Court and Constitutional Democracy*, Ithaca, NY: Cornell University Press, 1984.

Cox, Archibald, *The Court and the Constitution,* New York, NY: Houghton-Mifflin, 1988.

Dumbauld, Edward, *The Bill of Rights and What It Means Today,* New York, NY: Greenwood Press, 1979.

Goode, Stephen, *The Controversial Court: Supreme Court Influences on American Life,* New York, NY: Messner, 1982.

Lawson, Don, *Landmark Supreme Court Cases,* Hillside: Enslow Publishers, Inc., 1987.

Rehnquist, William H., *The Supreme Court: How It Was, How It Is,* New York, NY: Morrow, 1987.

Woodward, Bob, and Scott Armstrong, *The Brethren: Inside the Supreme Court,* New York, NY: Simon & Schuster, 1979.

Yudof, Mark, *When Government Speaks: Politics, Law, and Government Expression in America,* Berkeley, CA: University of California Press, 1983.

INDEX

EXCELLENT BOOKS ORDER FORM

(Please xerox this form so it will be available to other readers.)

Please send
Copy(ies)
_____ of LANDMARK DECISIONS I @ $16.95
_____ of LANDMARK DECISIONS II @ $16.95
_____ of LANDMARK DECISIONS III @ $16.95
_____ of LANDMARK DECISIONS IV @ $16.95
_____ of LANDMARK DECISIONS V @ $16.95
_____ of LANDMARK DECISIONS VI @ $16.95
_____ of SCHOOLHOUSE DECISIONS @ $16.95
_____ of LIFE, DEATH, AND THE LAW @ $16.95
_____ of FREEDOM OF SPEECH DECISIONS @ $16.95
_____ of FREEDOM OF THE PRESS DECISIONS @ $16.95
_____ of FREEDOM OF RELIGION DECISIONS @ $16.95
_____ of THE MURDER REFERENCE @ $16.95
_____ of THE RAPE REFERENCE @ $16.95
_____ of ABORTION DECISIONS: THE 1970's @ $16.95
_____ of ABORTION DECISIONS: THE 1980's @ $16.95
_____ of ABORTION DECISIONS: THE 1990's @ $16.95
_____ of CIVIL RIGHTS DECISIONS: 19th CENTURY@ $16.95
_____ of CIVIL RIGHTS DECISIONS: 20th CENTURY @ $16.95
_____ of THE ADA HANDBOOK @ $16.95

Name: _____

Address: _____

City: _____ State: _____ Zip: _____

Add $1 per book for shipping and handling.
California residents add sales tax.

OUR GUARANTEE: Any Excellent Book may be returned at
any time for any reason and a full refund will be made.

Mail your check or money order to: Excellent Books,
Post Office Box 131322, Carlsbad, California 92013-1322
or call/fax: (760) 598-5069 or e-mail us at: xlntbks@aol.com